Quick and Easy
GARDEN
Cross Stitch

Quick and Easy
GARDEN
Cross Stitch

Anne and Michael Lane

Michael O'Mara Books

First published in Great Britain in 1995 by
Michael O'Mara Books Limited
9 Lion Yard
Tremadoc Road
London SW4 7NQ

A CIP catalogue record for this book is available from the British Library

ISBN 1-85479-907-X (hardback)
ISBN 1-85479-641-0 (paperback)

1 3 5 7 9 10 8 6 4 2

Designed and Typeset by Clive Dorman & Co
Photographs by Helen Pask

Printed and bound by Mohndruck, Gütersloh, Germany

$\mathscr{C}$ontents

The Basics of Cross Stitch

THE FABRIC

To work cross stitch embroidery you need to use a material which has a regular and definite weave so that you can stitch your crosses easily. You will find that there are several types which are readily available, and we have used four for the projects in this book.

1 Cotton aida

This fabric is the one most commonly used for working cross stitch and you should be able to obtain it from any needlecraft supplier. It is a regularly woven fabric which looks like small squares with a hole at each corner, and your crosses are stitched by simply working from hole to hole diagonally across the square. Aida is available in many colours and is an extremely versatile material.

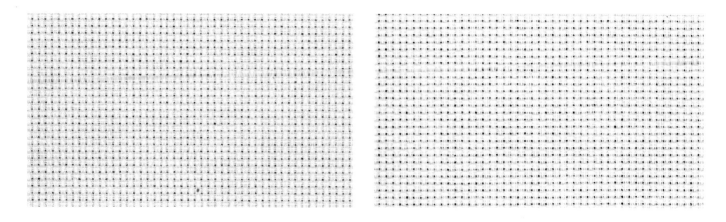

Cotton aidas

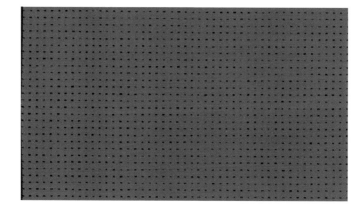

Many beginners' projects will use cotton aida as it is probably the easiest fabric on which to learn. It is referred to by the number of squares (and, therefore, stitches) to the inch and, of course, the more squares there are the finer the weave will be, with the fabric becoming slightly more difficult to work. The most commonly available fabrics are 14 count aida, which is used in many projects and kits, and 18 count aida, which is used to achieve more detail in delicate designs.

There are several other sizes of aida, from 5 count upwards (very good for young children!), but you may find that many aida-type fabrics will be referred to by specific trade names.

2 Evenweave fabrics

These fabrics are very different from aida because they are not solid weaves, but consist of threads of material regularly spaced across the length and breadth of the fabric, with crosses usually being made by working diagonally across two threads (see also The Stitches below). Some evenweave materials are available in different colours, but you will usually be required to work on white or natural colours, including the 'antique' dyes, which are popular in reproducing historical pieces.

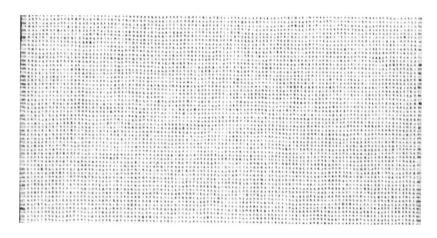

Evenweave fabrics

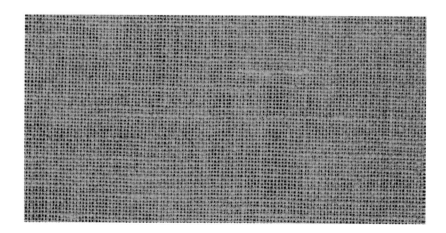

'Evenweave' in both cotton and linen can be obtained from a good supplier, but the range available may well be limited. The most common weave is around 26 threads to the inch (approximately equivalent to 14 count aida), though for some finer work you will find that 28 or 32 threads to the inch is used. This type of fabric, especially even-weave linen, is more traditional than aida and will be found used in older embroideries and samplers.

Evenweave fabrics are a little more difficult to work initially, but do not be discouraged, because once you are familiar with them you will find them just as easy to stitch as cotton aida.

3 Perforated paper
This is a stiffened craft paper that has holes punched in it through which your stitches are worked. Perforated paper corresponds very closely to 14 count aida in size, and is worked in exactly the same way, although you will need to use more strands of cotton in your needle to cover the paper completely. It is very useful for stitching articles that should not lose their shape when handled, and we have used it, for example, to make a bookmark and some Christmas decorations.

Perforated paper can be found in good needlework retailers, but if you have difficulty obtaining it, please refer to the list of suppliers at the end of the book.

4 Fine canvas
Canvas is, of course, usually associated with tapestry or needlepoint work, but fine canvas (we use 18 holes to the inch) is very good for stitching projects that require a more sturdy finish, such as the purse and the spectacle case to be found in the book. It should be readily available from any needlecraft supplier.

Canvas is worked in a slightly different way from the other three materials we have used (see The Stitches, below) and, as in tapestry work, the background will always be filled in with a solid colour so that no unworked canvas can be seen in the finished article. Projects using canvas can, therefore, take a little longer to complete.

PREPARING YOUR FABRIC TO START
To make sure that your embroidery is correctly positioned when you are stitching it, you will need to be certain that it is in the right place on your fabric. It is, therefore, extremely important to know where to work the first stitch, and because one of the golden rules of cross stitch embroidery is that you begin as close as you can to the centre of the design, what you need, in fact, is a simple method of determining where the centre of the design should be.

Unless your project states otherwise, the centre of the design will be at the centre of the fabric, and if this is so, then just follow these steps to find your starting point:

1   Fold your fabric in half along one side, and pinch gently to mark the central thread.
2   Tack some brightly coloured sewing cotton across the fabric following the line of this thread. This cotton is referred to as a 'guideline'.
3   Repeat this process along the second side of the fabric.
4   The point where your guidelines cross will mark the centre of the fabric, and the point where your centre stitch should be positioned.

Where a project calls for you to position the centre of the design away from the centre

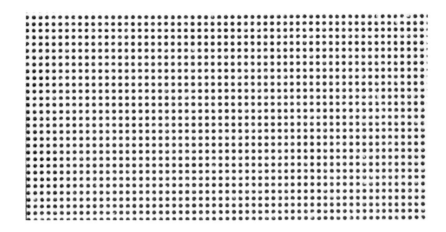

Perforated paper

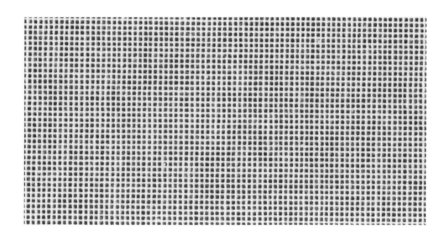

Fine canvas

of the fabric there will be specific instructions to follow and you will need to tack guide-lines along the threads indicated by the instructions rather than along central threads.

After stitching your guidelines always press the fabric carefully before you start the project, and, especially if you are using an evenweave material, it is advisable to hem around the edges so that they do not fray.

> *Hint:*
> Never remove your tacking until the project is finished, because you can use the guide-lines as helpful reference points when you are working.

USING AN EMBROIDERY HOOP OR TAPESTRY FRAME

It is perfectly possible to stitch many projects without using either an embroidery hoop or a tapestry frame, but it will be much easier to keep your stitches even and result in a neater finished piece if one is used.

Embroidery hoops

Embroidery hoops come in many sizes and are suitable for smaller designs, but you should make sure that the design fits completely inside the hoop without having to alter its position.

Traditional hoops are wooden and consist of two rings, one inside the other, with an adjustable screw attachment on the outer ring which is tightened to hold your fabric in place. You will also find plastic hoops which clip together to secure the fabric.

To fix your fabric in a wooden hoop:

1 After tacking the guidelines, place the fabric over the inner ring so that the centre of the design is in the centre of the ring, and with the tension screw loosened press the outer ring over it.
2 Smooth the fabric and, if necessary, straighten the weave before tightening the screw.
3 Fix your fabric securely enough to keep it taut, but do not stretch it too much as it is easy to distort the weave.

> **Hint:**
> To stop your fabric being marked by the friction of the hoop, lay tissue paper over it before fixing it in the outer ring. When you have tightened the screw you can tear the paper away from the area to be embroidered.

Tapestry frames

Tapestry frames should be used if the design is too big to fit a hoop, and there are many different types available including hand-held and floor-standing variations; if in doubt we advise you to talk to your supplier about your requirements. Frames usually comprise two rollers, with tapes attached, and two flat pieces which hold the rollers a set distance apart.

Using a tapestry frame

1 After marking the guidelines, fix your fabric to the tapes on both rollers with basting stitches and then oversew the tapes and fabric together, keeping the fabric flat but undistorted.
2 Hem the sides of your fabric to stop them fraying on the rollers.
3 Fit the side pieces, and gather up any extra fabric on to the rollers until the fabric is taut and you can easily see the area you wish to work.
4 Never leave worked fabric wound tightly on to a frame for long periods as the stitching will become flattened and lifeless.
5 If your piece of material is too small to fit the frame, you can make it larger by basting off-cuts of the same type of fabric to the top and bottom of your material and then fixing these to the frame.

THE COLOURS

Stranded embroidery cotton is the thread most commonly used in cross stitch embroidery. It is bought in skeins about 8 metres long, and there are several ranges readily obtainable. Throughout this book we have referred to the DMC range of colours, but a Conversion Table to other ranges will be found on p.125.

When you buy the cotton you will see that it is made up of six strands. You will almost always have to separate out these strands to use a smaller number when you are stitching. Most embroidery is worked with only two strands of cotton in the needle, but a particular project may use, for example, one or three strands, particularly for back-stitching (see The Stitches, below). Stitching on canvas and perforated paper is always worked with three strands.

It is very important that you are sure of how many strands you should be using. One of the most common errors made by beginners is to use the wrong number of strands when stitching.

Separating the strands

Cut off a length of between 18" and 24" from the skein and fold it loosely in half in your hand. Gently take hold of the number of strands you need, and starting at the centre, tease them completely away from the others and thread them through your needle. (Remember to use up the remaining strands from this length before cutting any more from the skein.)

Hint:
Store your unused working lengths of cotton on an organizer card, which you can also use for easy reference while you are stitching.

Take a piece of thin white card about 4" x 2" and make holes down each side about ½" apart to thread your cottons through. Label each colour with its number and you will not have to worry about matching the cut lengths to their skeins.

THE NEEDLE

You must use blunt-ended tapestry needles for cross stitch embroidery. Size 24 is suitable for most projects, but you will need the smaller size 26 on finer fabrics and for detailed work such as outlining.

Hint:
If the thread becomes very twisted when you are stitching, allow the needle to hang freely from the underside of the fabric to untwist it naturally.

THE STITCHES

The greatest attraction of cross stitch embroidery for many people is that although only a very few stitches have to be learnt, so many different effects can be achieved with them. Very basic and simple projects use the same stitches as the most complex and detailed of cross stitch embroideries, and once you have mastered the stitches explained below you will be able to work almost every cross stitch design.

Cross stitch

This stitch is, of course, the basis of all cross stitch embroidery. It is a very simple stitch to work, but to ensure that your finished piece is as attractive as possible you should make a particular effort to keep the tension of your stitches even – never pull too tight!

Making a single cross in cotton aida or evenweave:

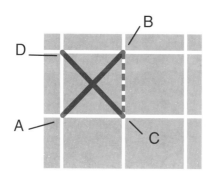 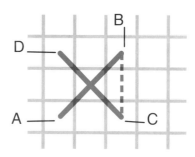

1   Bring your needle through at A and go back into the fabric at B. As you can see, this will be a diagonal across one square on cotton aida, or a diagonal across two threads of evenweave.
2   Move to C and bring your needle through once again, before completing the cross at D.

You will need to work in single stitches if the design requires you to do one of the following:
   a) to stitch a colour in a vertical line
   b) to stitch a colour diagonally
   c) to work individual stitches at random in order to provide detail

Make sure that after completing each stitch you begin the next one in the right place to complete your cross in the same way.

Working a row of cross stitches on cotton aida or evenweave:
When you have large areas of colour to fill you may find it easier to stitch in horizontal rows. The method below produces neat vertical lines on the reverse of the embroidery, making it easier to stretch when you have finished.

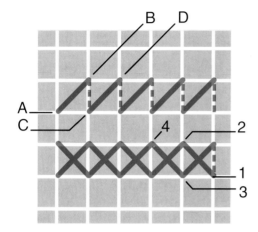 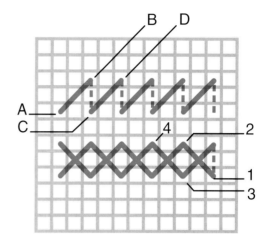

1   Work the first half of your crosses as shown (A to B, C to D, etc) until you have counted off the number of stitches in the row.
2   Make the crosses by returning along the row in reverse (1 to 2, 3 to 4, etc).

When you have completed one row move to a starting position which will allow you to work the next row in the same way.

NB The method of forming a cross which we have shown here is the one that we use, but you may prefer to work your stitch in reverse, so that the 'top' of the cross is stitched in the opposite direction. Whichever you choose, always make sure that the 'top' of EVERY stitch in the design is stitched in the SAME direction.

Hint:
When you are stitching do not start or end your threads by knotting them behind the fabric, as this produces a very uneven surface on the finished piece.
   To start stitching, hold about an inch of colour in place at the back and work your first few stitches over it to anchor it in position, and then, when you have come to the end of your section or your length, weave an inch or so of cotton into the back of existing stitches.

Cross stitches on perforated paper are worked in the same way as cross stitches on cotton aida, but using three strands of cotton.

Working cross stitches on canvas:
The crosses are formed as they are on the other types of material, but instead of working over two threads, you only work over one intersection of canvas, using three strands of cotton. This ensures that the canvas is completely covered.

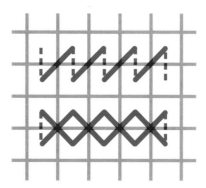

Back-stitch
Almost all projects will require you to provide extra definition to parts of the design by using simple back-stitch. This process is commonly known as outlining or, occasionally, overstitching.

NEVER start to do any back-stitching until you have completed ALL the cross stitches in a design.

The outlining will normally be shown by a continuous line on the chart (see The Design Chart, below) and you will need to follow this line exactly. It will often go over the top of cross stitches, and you must be certain of the number of strands you should have in your needle as this may well vary, not only from one project to another, but also within the same project. The colour you need for each part of the outlining will be indicated in the instructions accompanying a design.

Working back-stitch

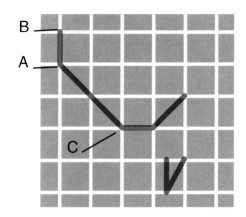
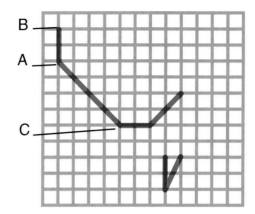

1 Start by anchoring your thread in the back of some cross stitches and then bring your needle through the fabric at a convenient point along the line (A).
2 Go back through the fabric at the beginning of the line (B).
3 Take your needle forward behind the material to another point on the line (C).
4 Bring your needle through at C and take it back again through A.
5 Continue in this way until you reach the end of the line, and then anchor your cotton into the backs of cross stitches.

> **Hint:**
> It is often more effective to work in longer back-stitches when you are outlining over the top of cross stitches, but never make them too long or they will become very loose.

Half cross stitches and threequarter cross stitches

As their names indicate, these stitches are based on a cross stitch, but are not worked as full crosses:

A half cross stitch is completed when the first half of the cross has been stitched. It is shown on a chart as a diagonal line, and your stitch should be worked in the same direction as the diagonal line.

A threequarter cross stitch is completed by working the first half of a cross, and then attaching a short diagonal from the centre into an opposite corner. The stitch is used to achieve a diagonal effect in a particular area of a design and is quite common, but it will only be found on more complex designs, and there are no threequarter cross stitches in this book.

THE DESIGN CHART

In cross stitch embroidery there is no transfer pattern on the fabric for you to follow. You must stitch your design by reference to a chart which will act as your blueprint. The important point to remember is that your stitching should correspond exactly to the design drawn on the chart.

Full-colour charts are used in this book, but you will also find many black-and-white charts in use. All charts are drawn on squared paper, with the position of every cross stitch on a colour chart being shown by a coloured square representing the colour you must use, whilst in a black-and-white chart the colour is shown by a symbol. A Colour Key accompanies each chart explaining the use of colours and symbols.

An empty square on the chart means that no stitch is to be worked in that square.

When following colour charts, an important point to realise is that the chart is not intended to be a painting of the design; it is a clear plan of the design devised to be as easy to follow as possible. You will, therefore, often find that where cotton colours are very close, a symbol has been added to some of the coloured squares to avoid confusion, and that the colours shown on the chart do not match the cottons exactly.

Outside the design on the chart there are arrows or some similar indication showing the central threads of the design. If you join these points in pencil across the chart itself you will be able to pinpoint the centre of the design exactly, and so position your first stitch on the fabric by reference to your guidelines.

> *Hint:*
> To use your organizer card as effectively as possible, you can make a note beside each colour of any symbol that is used to represent it on the chart. This will save you from some unnecessary searching through the Colour Key.

The shape of any back-stitching in a design is shown by a continuous line on the chart. If more than one colour is used for outlining in a project, then the details will be found in accompanying instructions and each colour used for back-stitching will be drawn using a different colour line. In order to show clearly on charts, the colour of back-stitching is often very different from the actual colour used, so do not be surprised if black cotton is represented by a red line!

On black-and-white charts it is more difficult to work out the positioning of back-stitching, but you will often find that different colours are represented by different types of line.

> *Hint:*
> Some people are discouraged from taking up cross stitch because they feel that charts look difficult to follow, and that it is easy to lose track of your position. You can stop this happening quite simply if you use a pin to show where you are!
> On a large design you may also wish to block in the areas of stitching that you have completed.

STITCHING THE DESIGN

The key to successful cross stitch embroidery lies in careful preparation and a complete understanding of the charts and techniques. When you are stitching there are only a few very simple rules to remember, and if you follow them closely your embroideries will be successful and attractive:

1 Start stitching at or near the centre of the design, and make sure that your first stitch is in the correct position on the fabric.
2 Work outwards from the centre so that you have to do as little counting as possible. When you have finished one section, always try to move on to an adjoining section.
3 If you do have to move across unstitched fabric, count off the number of stitches accurately. Take particular care to do this when you are using an evenweave material.
4 Work the largest areas of colour first, and fill in the detail later. Your embroidery will take shape more quickly, and it will be much easier to see exactly where your single stitches should go.
5 Keep the tension of your stitches as even as you can. Pull them firmly to avoid looping, but take care not to pull so tightly that you distort the weave of the fabric.
6 Complete all cross stitches (and any others in the design) before you start any outlining.
7 Do not trail lengths of cotton behind fabric that will remain unworked, as they may well show through the piece when it is finished.
8 Enjoy yourself.

> *Hint:*
> Although it is possible to hand-wash embroideries when they have been worked, it is not advisable to do so. It is far better to keep your work clean by always placing it in a clear plastic bag or something similar when you are not stitching.
> Stop the surface of finished embroideries becoming dirty by spraying them with a suitable fabric protector.

WHEN YOU HAVE FINISHED

Cross stitch embroidery is put to many uses, and in this book we have designed projects which will enable you to learn the most common methods of finishing off smaller pieces of work so that they are displayed to the best advantage. If you ever need, for example, to place your embroidery in a card, or turn it into a bookmark, you will find an example of how to do it in the following pages.

A word of warning, though. After you have stitched a large sampler or worked a beautiful fire-screen, do please go to a specialist framer who is experienced in mounting embroidery to seek advice. The craft of stretching large pieces of work properly is a skilled one, and takes much practice.

Kingfisher Picture

*V*ery rarely, when it is very quiet, this sleek and elegant bird can be glimpsed at rest, sunning himself on a branch overhanging the river. Work this colourful design and then mount it for all to see in the hoop that you have used to stitch it

YOU WILL NEED:
Design size: 3½" x 3¼" approx

To stitch the design:
5" traditional wooden embroidery hoop
10" x 10" of white cotton aida (14 count)
1 x 8m skein of DMC stranded embroidery cotton in
    each of the 14 colours listed in the Colour Key
Size 24 tapestry needle
Coloured cotton for marking the guidelines

To display the finished piece:
10" x 10" of white felt
White sewing cotton
Sharp sewing needle
Scissors
Fabric glue (optional)

STITCHING THE DESIGN:
1   Tack guidelines with coloured cotton to mark the
    centre of the aida before positioning it on your hoop.
2   Join the arrows on the chart to find the centre of the
    design, and stitch the piece using 2 strands of cotton
    for all cross stitches. Outlining details are included with
    the Colour Key.
3   Remove the aida from the hoop (do not take out the
    guidelines!) and steam press the worked piece flat after
    placing it face-down on a clean surface. If you are not
    using a steam iron, place a damp cloth over the wrong
    side of the aida before pressing it.

DISPLAYING THE PIECE:
1   Use the outside of the hoop's inner ring as a template
    to cut out a circle of white felt, which will act as your
    backing.
2   Replace the design centrally in the hoop using the
    guidelines to help you position it correctly.
3   Take out the guidelines.
4   Trim away excess aida from behind the hoop, leaving
    about 1" all around.
5   Work a row of running stitches in white cotton about
    ½" from the cut edge of the fabric, and gather them
    tightly before tying off the thread. The aida should
    now be lying within the thickness of your hoop.
6   Place the white felt circle over the back of the hoop,
    making sure it lies as flat as possible on the inner ring.
7   Fix the felt to the aida, using either a suitable glue or a
    few stitches worked around the edge.

COLOUR KEY							
⊟		BLANC		⧆	943	Bright Jade	
⊡	310	Black		⧆	991	Dark Jade	
9	317	Dark Grey		1	992	Jade Green	
2	318	Grey		Ⅲ	993	Pale Jade	
⠿	351	Coral Pink		7	3022	Dark Stone	
⊟	436	Golden Tan		5	3024	Stone	
3	738	Pale Tan		⧄		1 strand of 991 with	
4	798	Cobalt Blue				1 strand of 992	

OUTLINING

Use 1 strand of 310 Black around the eye
Use 1 strand of 317 Dark Grey at the neck

Country Pot Holder

❦

You'll be amazed how easy it is to make this useful holder decorated with marjoram from the herb garden

YOU WILL NEED:
to make one potholder, finished size 6" x 6" approx

To stitch the design:
8" x 8" of white cotton aida (14 count)
1 x 8m skein of DMC stranded embroidery cotton in
    each of the 6 colours listed in the Colour Key
Size 24 tapestry needle
Coloured cotton for marking the guidelines

To make the potholder:
7" x 7" of a quilted backing fabric of your choice
1 yd of green bias binding (⅝" wide)
Green sewing cotton to match your binding
Sharp sewing needle
Pins
Scissors

STITCHING THE DESIGN:
1   Tack guidelines with coloured cotton to mark the
    centre of the aida before positioning it on your hoop or
    frame. This design will fit into a 6" embroidery hoop.
2   Join the arrows on the chart to find the centre of the
    design, and stitch the piece using 2 strands of cotton
    for all cross stitches. No back-stitching is required.
3   Remove the guidelines and steam press the worked
    piece flat after placing it face-down on a clean surface.
    If you are not using a steam iron, place a damp cloth
    over the wrong side of the aida before pressing it.

MAKING THE POTHOLDER:
1   Turn the design face-up, and trim the aida fabric to
    7" x 7", ensuring that the design remains centrally
    positioned.
2   Turn the design face-down and lay the quilted fabric
    on top of it.
3   Join the fabrics together by basting stitches all around,
    taking a ½" seam from every side. Hand or machine-
    stitch along the seam and then remove the basting.
4   Trim the seam allowance to ¼" wide.
5   Attach the bias binding to the potholder (*see 8 below*),
    starting at the top left-hand corner of the aida, and
    continuing around all sides. When you have returned
    to your starting-point, measure another 2¼" of binding
    before cutting off the excess.
6   Slip-stitch the long edges of this extra binding together,
    and then form a loop, folding the raw end under about
    ¼".
7   Fix the loop to the quilted side of the potholder, using
    small stitches for the best result.
8   **To attach bias binding:**
a) Open out the turning on one edge of the binding,
    and pin it in position on the right side of the fabric,
    matching the edge of the binding to the raw edges of
    the seam allowance(s). Secure the binding by hand or
    machine-stitching along the seamline(s) and remove
    the pins.
b) Fold the binding over the raw edges on to the wrong
    side of the fabric, and hold it in position with pins or
    basting stitches before neatly hemming it to finish.
    Make sure that you remove all pins and basting
    stitches.

COLOUR KEY					
⊟	597	Turquoise	1	704	Bright Leaf Green
Ⅱ	598	Pale Turquoise	3	962	Carmine Rose Pink
2	701	Dark Bright Green	4	3350	Old Carmine Rose

Cameo Collection

Starting with the same, simple design you can create a beautiful jewellery collection if you use a variety of rich and vibrant backgrounds

YOU WILL NEED:

to make one brooch or pendant, finished size 1⅝" x 1½" approx

(The chart shows three variations of the design with different backgrounds. Each design will fit any of the brooch mounts.)

To stitch the design once:

5" x 5" white single thread interlock canvas (18 holes to the inch)
1 x 8m skein of DMC stranded embroidery cotton in 5 of the colours listed in the Colour Key
Size 26 tapestry needle
Coloured cotton for marking the guidelines

To assemble a brooch or pendant:

3" x 3" of medium-weight iron-on white interfacing
White card
Pins
Scissors
Black background as shown: 1⅝" x 1³⁄₁₆" Antique Gold frame
Mauve background as shown: 1⅝" x 1¼" Gilding Metal brooch
Old Rose Pink pendant: 1⅝" x 1¼" Golden frame 24" gilt chain
For suppliers of the brooch mounts and gilt chain, see p.124

STITCHING THE DESIGN ONCE:

1 Tack guidelines with coloured cotton to mark the centre of the canvas. You should find that the canvas is stiff enough to work it in your hand, but you may wish to fix it to a small tapestry frame. Do not use an embroidery hoop!
2 Join the arrows on the chart to find the centre of the design, and stitch the piece using 3 strands of cotton for all cross stitches. No back-stitching is required.
3 Stitch each cross stitch over one intersection of canvas only (see The Basics of Cross Stitch, p.14).
4 Remove the guidelines and gently ease the worked piece flat and square by pulling at each corner. You should not use steam on canvas unless it has been properly 'blocked' by a professional stretcher.

ASSEMBLING A BROOCH OR PENDANT:

1 With the design face-down, iron the interfacing on to the wrong side of the canvas, making sure that you cover all the stitching. The interfacing adds stability to the canvas and also prevents stitches from fraying when you trim the design to fit the brooch mount.
2 Use the acetate provided with the mount to draw a template which can be used to trim the design to the correct size. Place the acetate on white card and draw around it in pencil.
3 Cut out the template around the inside edge of the pencil line and then pin it securely on top of your design so that the same amount of stitching shows on all sides.
4 Trim around the template as carefully as you can.
5 Finish assembling the brooch or pendant by following the supplier's instructions.

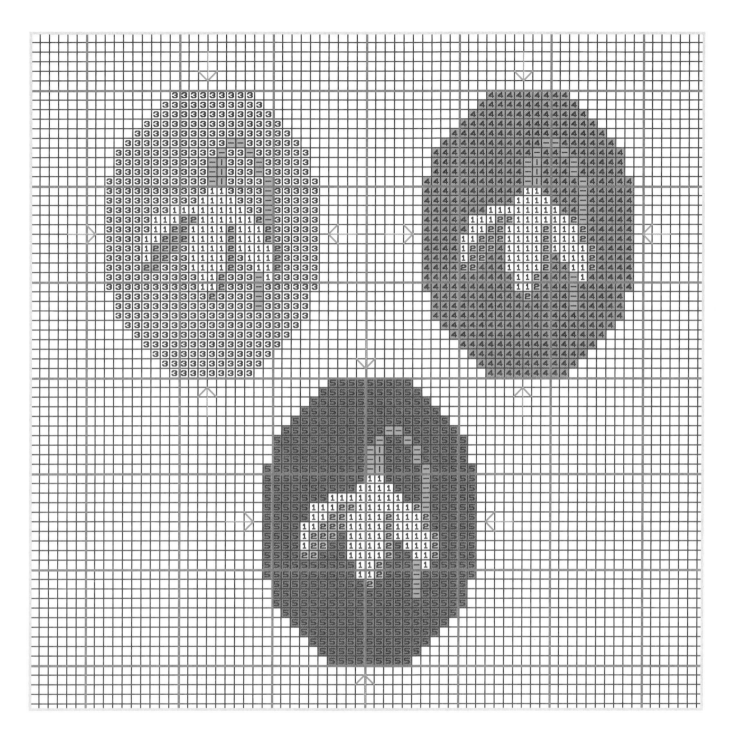

COLOUR KEY					
1		BLANC	▯	700	Dark Emerald Green
3	310	Black	▬	702	Emerald Green
5	327	Mauve	4	956	Old Rose Pink
2	415	Pale Grey			

CAMEO COLLECTION **29**

Christmas Card

Embroidered cards mean so much to those who receive them, and they are very easy to make – why not try this winter scene to start with?

YOU WILL NEED:

to make one card, with a design size 2½" x 2" approx

To stitch the design:

6" x 6" of white cotton aida (18 count)
1 x 8m skein of DMC stranded embroidery cotton in
  each of the 13 colours listed in the Colour Key
Size 26 tapestry needle
Coloured cotton for marking the guidelines

To assemble the card:

6" x 6" of medium-weight iron-on white interfacing
Double-sided tape (½" wide)
Three-leaved card mount with aperture 3½" x 3" approx
Scissors

STITCHING THE DESIGN:

1 Tack guidelines with coloured cotton to mark the
   centre of the aida before positioning it on your hoop
   or frame. This design will fit into a 5" embroidery
   hoop.
2 Join the arrows on the chart to find the centre of the
   design, and stitch the piece using 2 strands of cotton
   for all cross stitches. Outlining details are included
   with the Colour Key.
3 Remove the guidelines and steam press the worked
   piece flat after placing it face-down on a clean surface.
   If you are not using a steam iron, place a damp cloth
   over the wrong side of the aida before pressing it.

ASSEMBLING THE CARD:

1 After pressing your worked piece, leave it face-down
   and iron the interfacing on to it to provide necessary
   stiffening.
2 Place the aperture of the card over the design, and, if
   necessary, trim the stiffened aida to size. Keep the
   design centrally-positioned, and cut the fabric so that
   it overlaps the aperture by at least ¾" on each side.
3 Put strips of double-sided tape around the inside of
   the card, near to each edge of the aperture, and then
   position the taped side of the card over the design and
   press it down on to the fabric. Do not press too firmly
   until you are sure that your design is in the right
   place.
4 Lay the design face-down, with the holly nearest to
   you, and fix strips of double-sided tape on the left-
   hand leaf of the card. Press this tape firmly down on
   to the central leaf to hide the aida.

COLOUR KEY					
7		BLANC	6	642	Dark Stone
1	310	Black	9	702	Emerald Green
3	318	Grey	10	703	Bright Leaf Green
4	420	Wood Brown	2	712	Pale Linen
5	422	Cinnamon	—	947	Orange Coral
8	434	Dark Wood Brown	11	3341	Coral
—	608	Orange Flame			

OUTLINING

Use 1 strand of 310 Black for the beak and around the eye

Use 1 strand of 318 Grey around the snow on top of the post

Summertime
Picture

❦

In the still, hazy heat of
midsummer a tortoiseshell butterfly
flutters gently towards a clump of wild
flowers, preparing to alight
undisturbed…

YOU WILL NEED:
Design size 3½" x 3½" approx

To stitch the design:
10" x 10" of white cotton aida (14 count)
1 x 8m skein of DMC stranded embroidery cotton in
    each of the 15 colours listed in the Colour Key and
    Outlining
Size 24 tapestry needle
Coloured cotton for marking the guidelines

To mount the embroidery:
5½" x 5½" of white mounting board
Pins
Double-sided tape (½" wide)
Masking tape (1" wide)

STITCHING THE DESIGN:
1 Tack guidelines with coloured cotton to mark the
    centre of the aida before positioning it on your hoop
    or frame. This design requires an embroidery hoop of
    at least 6".
2 Join the arrows on the chart to find the centre of the
    design, and stitch the piece using 2 strands of cotton
    for all cross stitches. Outlining details are included
    with the Colour Key.
3 Do not remove the guidelines, but steam press the
    worked piece flat after placing it face-down on a clean
    surface. If you are not using a steam iron, place a
    damp cloth over the wrong side of the aida before
    pressing it.

MOUNTING THE EMBROIDERY:
1 Trim the aida to 7½" x 7½", ensuring that the design
    remains centrally positioned.
2 With the design face-down, place the mounting board
    centrally over the aida. To do this, mark the mid-
    point on all four sides of the card, and align these
    points with the guidelines on your fabric.
3 Place a pin into the thickness of the board at each of
    these four points, joining the aida and the board
    together. Turn the board over so that you can see the
    embroidery.
4 Starting at the top of the design, place pins at regular
    intervals into the thickness of the board to stretch the
    aida. Work from the mid-point to each side, and keep
    the fabric as flat and square as you can. This is done
    by keeping the thread of aida nearest to the edge as
    straight as possible, and pulling the fabric so that it
    lies flat but does not distort.
5 Repeat the process around the other three sides of the
    design *(working top-side-bottom-side)*, but on these
    sides work from a pinned corner to the opposite
    corner. You may well find that your central pins will
    need to be moved as the embroidery is stretched.
6 When you have pinned all four sides, make any neces-
    sary adjustments, remove the guidelines, and place the
    design face-down.
7 Cut a strip of double-sided tape 5½" long, and lay it
    along the top edge of the board. Fold the aida over so
    that it is held securely by the tape and then repeat the
    process around the other three sides *(working top-
    bottom-side-side)*. The corners will have an extra thick-
    ness, but try to keep them as flat as you can.
8 Cover the raw edges of the fabric with strips of mask-
    ing tape and remove all pins.

This method of mounting embroidery is very suitable for
small designs such as those in this book. If you wish to
mount large designs, or embroideries worked on heavy-
weight fabrics, we recommend that the work is done by a
professional stretcher and framer who will probably use
lacing thread.

OUTLINING

Use 1 strand of 209 Dark Lilac around the flowers
Use 1 strand of 987 Dark Leaf Green for the leaf veins
Use 1 strand of 3031 Peat Brown for the butterfly's antennae
Use 1 strand of 420 Wood Brown around the edges of the wings

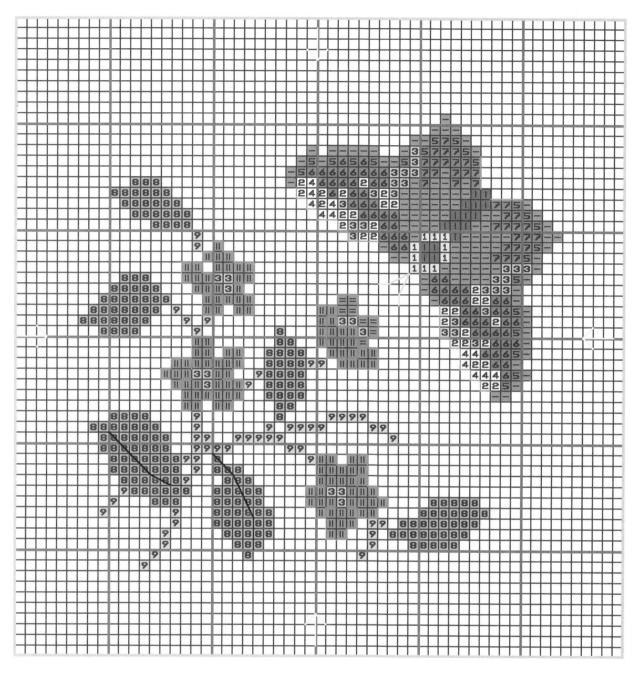

Strawberry Pincushion

Every stitcher needs a pincushion, so why not make your own? This most traditional of all accessories has been decorated with the strawberry, one of the oldest embroidered motifs, in use since medieval times

YOU WILL NEED:
to make one pincushion, finished size 3¾" x 3¾" approx

To stitch the design:
6" x 6" white single-thread interlock canvas (18 holes to the inch)

1 x 8m skein of DMC stranded embroidery cotton in each of the colours listed in the Colour Key, except shade 798 Cobalt Blue

4 x 8m skeins of DMC stranded embroidery cotton, shade 798 Cobalt Blue

Size 24 tapestry needle

Coloured cotton for marking the guidelines

To make the pincushion:
6" x 6" of blue velvet fabric

Wadding (eg kapok)

Blue sewing cotton to match your velvet

Sharp sewing needle

Pins

Scissors

STITCHING THE DESIGN:
1 Tack guidelines with coloured cotton to mark the centre of the canvas. You should find that the canvas is stiff enough to work it in your hand, but you may wish to fix it to a small tapestry frame. Do not use an embroidery hoop!

2 Join the arrows on the chart to find the centre of the design, and stitch the piece using 3 strands of cotton for all cross stitches. No back-stitching is required.

3 Stitch each cross stitch over one intersection of canvas only (see The Basics of Cross Stitch, p.14).

4 Remove the guidelines and gently ease the worked piece flat and square by pulling at each corner. You should not use steam on canvas unless it has been properly 'blocked' by a professional stretcher.

MAKING THE PINCUSHION:
1 Measure ½" away from the stitching on all four sides and trim the canvas to size. Cut the blue velvet to the same size by laying it on top of the canvas.

2 Place the two fabrics right sides together and join them with basting stitches all around, taking a ½" seam from every side. Leave an opening of about 2" along one side so that you can pad out the pincushion with wadding. Hand or machine-stitch along the seam and then remove the basting.

3 Trim the seam allowance close to the seam itself, and turn the pincushion right side out, making sure that the seams lie as flat as possible inside.

4 Insert wadding to the required firmness, and finish by slipstitching your opening closed along the stitching line.

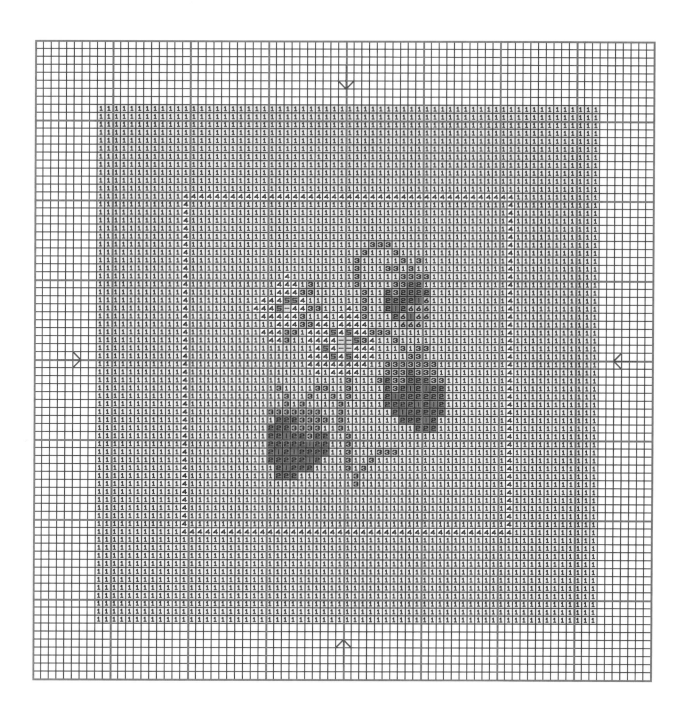

COLOUR KEY					
4		BLANC	3	703	Brilliant Green
1	351	Coral	5	740	Orange
6	352	Strawberry Pink	1	798	Cobalt Blue
2	606	Flame Red	−	973	Bright Yellow

Country Cottage Sampler

The most popular form of
decorative embroidery is the sampler –
this colourful and modern version is
inspired by the black and white
cottages of the Shropshire hills

YOU WILL NEED:
Design size 6½" x 5½" approx

To stitch the design:
12" x 11" of cream cotton aida (14 count)
1 x 8m skein of DMC stranded embroidery cotton in
    each of the 11 colours listed in the Colour Key
Size 24 tapestry needle
Coloured cotton for marking the guidelines

To mount the embroidery:
8½" x 7½" of white mounting board
Pins
Double-sided tape (1" wide)
Masking tape (1" wide)

STITCHING THE DESIGN:
1   Tack guidelines with coloured cotton to mark the
    centre of the aida before positioning it on your frame.
    This design does not fit comfortably into an embroi-
    dery hoop.
2   Join the arrows on the chart to find the centre of the
    design, and stitch the piece using 2 strands of cotton
    for all cross stitches. Outlining details are included
    with the Colour Key.
3   Do not remove the guidelines, but steam press the
    worked piece flat after placing it face-down on a clean
    surface. If you are not using a steam iron, place a
    damp cloth over the wrong side of the aida before
    pressing it.

MOUNTING THE EMBROIDERY:
1   Trim the aida to 10½" x 9½", ensuring that the design
    remains centrally positioned.
2   With the design face-down, place the mounting board
    centrally over the aida. To do this, mark the mid-
    point on all four sides of the card, and align these
    points with the guidelines on your fabric.
3   Place a pin into the thickness of the board at each of
    these four points, joining the aida and the board
    together. Turn the board over so that you can see the
    embroidery.
4   Starting at the top of the design, place pins at regular
    intervals into the thickness of the board to stretch the
    aida. Work from the mid-point to each side, and keep
    the fabric as flat and square as you can. This is done
    by keeping the thread of aida nearest to the edge as
    straight as possible, and pulling the fabric so that it
    lies flat but does not distort.
5   Repeat the process around the other three sides of the
    design *(working top-side-bottom-side)*, but on these
    sides work from a pinned corner to the opposite
    corner. You may well find that your central pins will
    need to be moved as the embroidery is stretched.
6   When you have pinned all four sides, make any neces-
    sary adjustments, remove the guidelines, and place the
    design face-down.
7   Cut a strip of double-sided tape 8½" long, and lay it
    along the top edge of the board. Fold the aida over so
    that it is held securely by the tape and then repeat the
    process around the other three edges *(working top-
    bottom-side-side)*, with the tape at the two sides being
    7½" long. The corners will have an extra thickness,
    but try to keep them as flat as you can.
8   Cover the raw edges of the fabric with strips of mask-
    ing tape and remove all pins.

This method of mounting embroidery is very suitable for
small designs such as those in this book. If you wish to
mount large designs, or embroideries worked on heavy-
weight fabrics, we recommend that the work is done by a
professional stretcher and framer who will probably use
lacing thread.

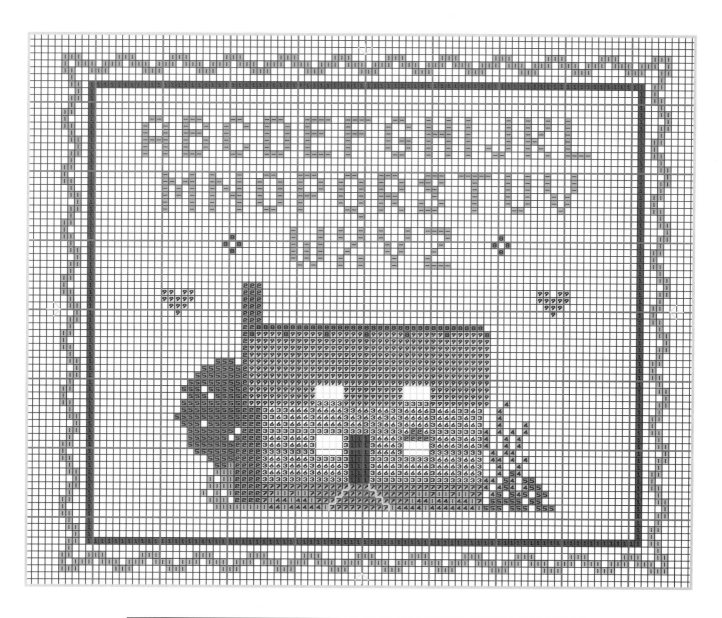

COLOUR KEY

6		BLANC	7	644	Dark Linen
–	210	Lilac	9	676	Golden Straw
3	310	Black	8	680	Dark Gold
4	351	Deep Coral	5	890	Dark Forest Green
I	367	Forest Green	2	3064	Brick
1	420	Wood Brown			

OUTLINING

Use 1 strand of 310 Black for all outlining on the cottage

Owl Bookmark

Using this bookmark will remind you of what it is that makes the owl so wise and respected – perhaps it can do the same for you!

YOU WILL NEED:
to make one bookmark, finished size 5½" x 2¾" approx, plus ribbon

To stitch the design:
7½" x 4½" of white perforated paper (14 holes to the inch). For suppliers see p.122
1 x 8m skein of DMC stranded embroidery cotton in each of the 13 colours listed in the Colour Key
Size 24 tapestry needle
Coloured cotton for marking the guidelines

To make the bookmark:
6" x 3" of medium-weight iron-on white interfacing
12" of double-sided green satin ribbon (½" wide)
Pins
Scissors

STITCHING THE DESIGN:
1 Tack guidelines with coloured cotton to mark the centre of the paper – you will need to do this by counting, as the paper must not be folded.
2 Work the design in your hand; do not use a hoop or frame.
3 Join the arrows on the chart to find the centre of the design, and stitch the piece using 3 strands of cotton for all cross stitches. Outlining details are included with the Colour Key.
4 Perforated paper does not require pressing. Remove the guidelines.

MAKING THE BOOKMARK:
1 Mark the cutting line on to the right side of the design, and carefully trim the bookmark to size.
2 Turn the design face-down and trim the interfacing so that there will be a border of one stitch of paper showing at each edge when the interfacing is ironed into place. Put the interfacing to one side.
3 Press the ribbon in half, and with the design face-down, pin it into position near to the bottom right-hand corner of the perforated paper, so that ½" of the ribbon will lie beneath the interfacing.
4 Iron the interfacing on to the wrong side of the paper, positioning it carefully. Make sure that the ribbon is securely fixed and then remove the pin.
5 Cut a small 'V' shape into each end of the ribbon streamer.

COLOUR KEY

II	301	Pale Chestnut Brown	7	612	Stone
6	310	Black	5	644	Dark Linen
9	400	Chestnut Brown	2	741	Bright Orange
1	436	Golden Tan	4	822	Linen
=	535	Dark Grey	−	3021	Dark Chocolate
3	610	Chocolate Brown	8	3033	Pale Stone
I	611	Stone Brown			

OUTLINING

Use 3 strands of 610 Chocolate Brown for all outlining
The red line on the chart indicates the cutting line

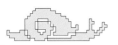

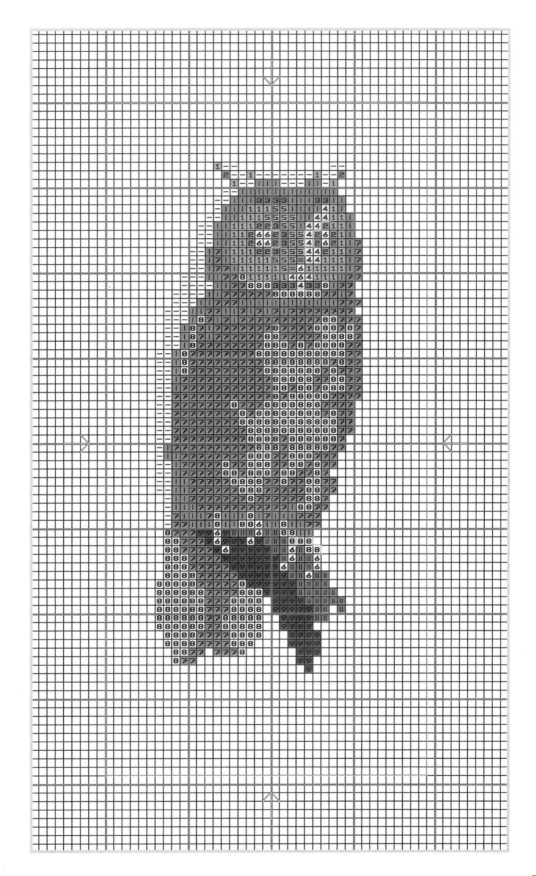

Honeypot Cover

Brighten up your morning with this miniature design which will bring the sights and sounds of summer to your breakfast table every day

YOU WILL NEED:

to make one cover, finished size 6" x 6" approx

To stitch the design:

8" x 8" of white cotton aida (18 count)

1 x 8m skein of DMC stranded embroidery cotton in each of the 10 colours listed in the Colour Key and Outlining

Size 26 tapestry needle

Coloured cotton for marking the guidelines

To make the cover:

White sewing cotton

Sharp sewing needle

Pins

Scissors

1lb jar of honey

Thin white elastic band

24" of narrow double-sided green satin ribbon

STITCHING THE DESIGN:

1   Tack guidelines with coloured cotton to mark the centre of the aida before positioning it on your hoop or frame. This design will fit into a 5" embroidery hoop.

2   Join the arrows on the chart to find the centre of the design, and stitch the piece using 2 strands of cotton for all cross stitches. Outlining details are included with the Colour Key.

3   Remove the guidelines and steam press the worked piece flat after placing it face-down on a clean surface. If you are not using a steam iron, place a damp cloth over the wrong side of the aida before pressing it.

MAKING THE COVER:

1   Measure 1" from the edge of the aida around all four sides, and tack new guidelines along the nearest threads.

2   Place pins at the four points where these guidelines cross and then remove the tacking.

3   Starting at a pin, work a square in blanket-stitch with the pins at each corner.

4   Remove the pins, and cut around the outside of the blanket-stitch, one aida square away from the stitching.

5   Place the design centrally over the lid of the honey jar and hold the fabric in place with the elastic band. If necessary, ease the aida gently so that it lies flat on the lid.

6   Tie the ribbon around the jar, making sure that it covers the elastic band completely.

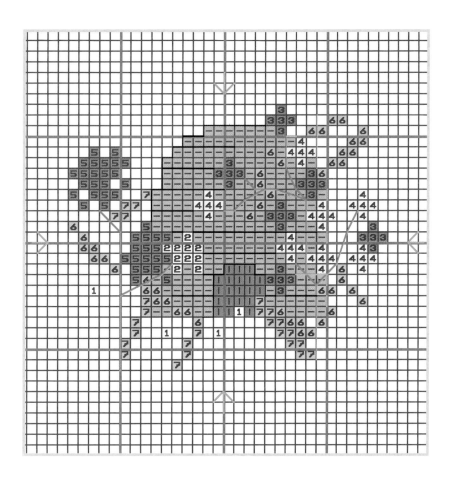

COLOUR KEY					
2		BLANC	6	701	Bright Green
1	310	Black	3	792	Deep Blue
5	351	Deep Coral	4	813	China Blue
I	434	Dark Wood Brown	7	966	Pale Laurel
−	437	Harvest Gold			

OUTLINING

— Use 1 strand of 434 Dark Wood Brown around the hive

— Use 1 strand of 699 Dark Bright Green for the flower stems

Christmas Tree Decorations

As Christmas draws near we gather the holly and the ivy from the hedgerows, and dig up the tree to bring it in once again. We hope these three colourful hanging decorations will add a sparkle to your celebrations

YOU WILL NEED:

to make three decorations, finished size 3" x 3" approx, plus ribbon

To stitch the design:

3 pieces of white perforated paper (14 holes to the inch) cut to 4½" x 4½". For suppliers see p.122

1 x 8m skein of DMC stranded embroidery cotton in each of the 2 colours listed in the Colour Key

Mez Diadem Gold Metallic Thread (shade 0300) or similar

Size 24 tapestry needle

Coloured cotton for marking the guidelines

To make the bookmark:

3 pieces of medium-weight iron-on white interfacing cut to 3" x 3"

3 yds of gold ribbon (⅛" or 3mm wide)

White cotton

Sharp sewing needle

Pins

Scissors

Double-sided tape (½" wide)

STITCHING THE DESIGNS:

1 Tack guidelines with coloured cotton to mark the centre of a piece of paper – you will need to do this by counting, as the paper must not be folded.

2 Work the design in your hand; do not use a hoop or frame.

3 Join the arrows on the chart to find the centre of the design, and stitch the piece using 3 strands of cotton for all cross stitches. There is no outlining with stranded cotton on these designs.

4 The metallic thread is worked in straight-stitch or half cross stitch as it is shown on the charts. Use the thread as provided, and make sure that it lies as flat as possible.

5 Perforated paper does not require pressing. Leave the guidelines in position.

MAKING EACH DECORATION:

1 Mark the cutting line on to the right side of the design, and carefully trim the decoration to size.

2 Turn the design face-down and trim the interfacing so that it slightly overlaps your stitching when it is ironed into place. Put the interfacing to one side.

3 Take 1 yd of ribbon and cut two lengths of 15" from it. Fold one piece of ribbon in half to form a loop, and catch the ends together with a stitch. Turn the design face-down and place the loop centrally at the top of the design so that its end will lie ½" beneath the interfacing. Hold it in position with a pin and remove the guidelines.

4 Iron the interfacing on to the back of the design, positioning it carefully. Make sure that the ribbon is securely fixed and then remove the pin.

5 Make a bow from the second length of ribbon and trim the ends to your chosen length.

6 Turn the design face-up, and place a small piece of double-sided tape centrally at the top of the paper (ie where the loop meets the paper). Press the bow firmly on to the tape.

COLOUR KEY					
■	606	Bright Red	‖	701	Bright Green

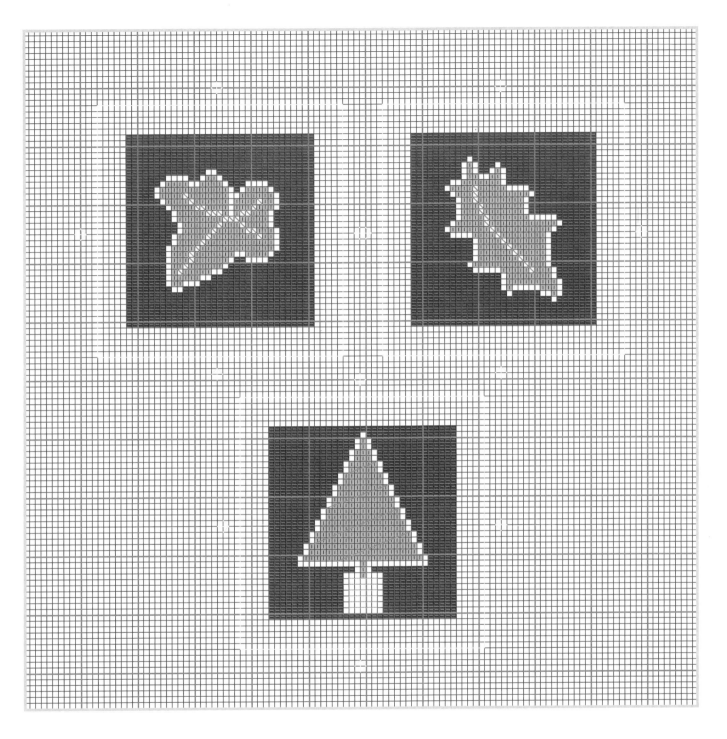

OUTLINING

- On the two leaves, work the Gold Metallic Thread as half cross stitches sloping in the direction indicated.
- On the tree, work the Gold Metallic Thread streamers as single straight stitches.

The tree tub is worked by stitching 6 horizontal straight stitches.

The yellow line on each chart indicates the cutting line.

Garden Picture

*A*mongst the rolling hills that
surround us, there is a secluded and
lonely spot where we can find the
luxuriant plants and brilliant colours
of the Mediterranean reflected
in the countryside…

YOU WILL NEED:
Design size 4½" x 2¼" approx

To stitch the design:
10" x 8" of white cotton aida (14 count)
1 x 8m skein of DMC stranded embroidery cotton in
    each of the 12 colours listed in the Colour Key
Size 24 tapestry needle
Coloured cotton for marking the guidelines

To mount the embroidery:
6½" x 4¼" of white mounting board
Pins
Double-sided tape (½" wide)
Masking tape (1" wide)

STITCHING THE DESIGN:
1 Tack guidelines with coloured cotton to mark the
   centre of the aida before positioning it on your hoop
   or frame. This design requires at least a 6" embroidery
   hoop.
2 Join the arrows on the chart to find the centre of the
   design, and stitch the piece using 2 strands of cotton
   for all cross stitches.
3 Do not remove the guidelines, but steam press the
   worked piece flat after placing it face-down on a clean
   surface. If you are not using a steam iron, place a
   damp cloth over the wrong side of the aida before
   pressing it.

MOUNTING THE EMBROIDERY:
1 Trim the aida to 8½". x 6¼", ensuring that the design
   remains centrally positioned.
2 With the design face-down, place the mounting board
   centrally over the aida. To do this, mark the mid-
   point on all four sides of the card, and align these
   points with the guidelines on your fabric.
3 Place a pin into the thickness of the board at each of
   these four points, joining the aida and the board
   together. Turn the board over so that you can see the
   embroidery.
4 Starting at the top of the design, place pins at regular
   intervals into the thickness of the board to stretch the
   aida. Work from the mid-point to each side, and keep
   the fabric as flat and square as you can. This is done
   by keeping the thread of aida nearest to the edge as
   straight as possible, and pulling the fabric so that it
   lies flat but does not distort.
5 Repeat the process around the other three sides of the
   design *(working top-side-bottom-side)*, but on these
   sides work from a pinned corner to the opposite
   corner. You may well find that your central pins will
   need to be moved as the embroidery is stretched.
6 When you have pinned all four sides, make any necessary adjustments, remove the guidelines, and place the
   design face-down.
7 Cut a strip of double-sided tape 6½" long, and lay it
   on the board along one of the sides. Fold the aida
   over so that it is held securely by the tape and then
   repeat the process around the other three sides *(working side-side-top-bottom)*, with the tape at the top and
   bottom being 4¼" long. The corners will have an
   extra thickness, but try to keep them as flat as you
   can.
8 Cover the raw edges of the fabric with strips of masking tape and remove all pins. The design will be
   shown to best effect in a picture mount which slightly
   overlaps the stitches around all four sides.

This method of mounting embroidery is very suitable for
small designs such as those in this book. If you wish to
mount large designs, or embroideries worked on heavy-
weight fabrics, we recommend that the work is done by a
professional stretcher and framer who will probably use
lacing thread.

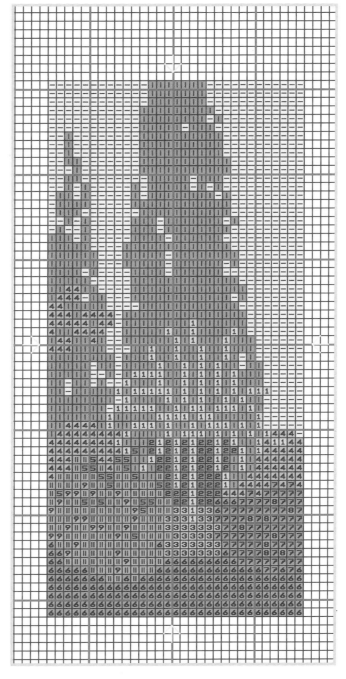

COLOUR KEY					
▯	367	Forest Green	🯲	922	Terracotta
🄸	369	Pale Forest Green	🯵	956	Old Rose
Ⅲ	470	Bright Green	🯶	989	Grass Green
⊟	747	Sky Blue	🯷	3345	Dark Green
🯹	772	Wood Green	🯴	3348	Moss Green
🯅	842	Stone	🯸	3609	Cyclamen

Keepsake Bag

⟡

This very simple version of a drawstring bag is an ideal place for keeping all those bits and pieces you can never find when you need them…

YOU WILL NEED:

to make one bag, finished size 6" x 4" approx

To stitch the design:

9" x 7¼" of white evenweave cotton (26 threads to the inch)

1 x 8m skein of DMC stranded embroidery cotton in each of the 9 colours listed in the Colour Key

Size 24 tapestry needle

Coloured cotton for marking the guidelines

To make the bag:

White sewing cotton

Sharp sewing needle

30" of thin white cording

Pins

Scissors

STITCHING THE DESIGN:

1 Place the evenweave so that its long side runs from left to right, and mark the vertical guideline of the design by measuring in 2½" from the right-hand edge and following the thread nearest to this point.

2 To mark the second guideline, measure up 2¾" from the bottom of the fabric and follow the nearest thread. The design is stitched in the right-hand half of the fabric only, with the point where your guide-lines cross being the point where the centre of the design is positioned.

3 If you fix this design to a hoop take particular care not to mark the fabric. It may be better to use a small tapestry frame.

4 Join the arrows on the chart to find the centre of the design, and stitch the piece using 2 strands of cotton for all cross stitches. Outlining details are included with the Colour Key.

5 Remove the guidelines and steam press the worked piece flat after placing it face-down on a clean surface. If you are not using a steam iron, place a damp cloth over the wrong side of the fabric before pressing it.

MAKING THE BAG:

1 Measure down ¾" from the top of the fabric and, following the nearest thread, mark a new guideline from left to right. Mark another guideline 1¼" from the top. These guidelines indicate the casing for your cording.

2 With the design face-up, fold the evenweave in half so that the right sides are together, with the stitched design being covered by the left-hand side of the fabric. All the working on this project is done on the wrong side.

3 Taking a ½" seam, join the side and bottom together with basting stitches, but leave the space between your two guidelines open. Hand or machine-stitch along the seam and remove the basting stitches. Trim the seam allowance to ¼".

4 Fold a small hem along a thread about ¼" from the top of your bag and press it flat.

5 Form the casing by folding over the new upper edge along your top guideline. Pin it in place, and remove both guidelines.

6 Stitch around the casing, working as close as you can to the pressed edge, and then turn the bag right side out. Take care that all seams lie as flat as possible.

7 Insert the cording into the casing, pulling the ends to an even length, and knot the ends together at a chosen point.

COLOUR KEY					
−	435	Golden Brown	2	891	Deep Pink
1	472	Pale Spring Green	3	956	Old Rose
6	552	Dark Violet	4	957	Fuchsia Pink
5	553	Violet	1	989	Leaf Green

OUTLINING

Use 1 strand of 956 Old Rose for the flower stamens

Use 1 strand of 987 Dark Leaf Green for the leaf veins

Valentine Gift

A heart to stitch as
a token of love; a treasure to
be kept for ever

YOU WILL NEED:
to make one heart, finished size 4½" x 4½" approx

To stitch the design:
8" x 8" of white evenweave cotton (26 threads to the inch)

1 x 8m skein of DMC stranded embroidery cotton in each of the 3 colours listed in the Colour Key

DMC Fil Or Clair [Gold Metallic Thread]

Size 24 tapestry needle

Coloured cotton for marking the guidelines

To make the heart:
2 pieces of plain white cotton fabric (eg cotton lawn), both 8" x 8"

7" of gold ribbon, ¼" wide

Wadding

White sewing cotton

Sharp sewing needle

Pins

Pinking shears

STITCHING THE DESIGN:
1   Tack guidelines with coloured cotton to mark the centre of the evenweave before positioning it on your hoop or frame. This design will fit into a 6" embroidery hoop.

2   Join the arrows on the chart to find the centre of the design, and stitch the piece using 2 strands of cotton for all cross stitches. Outlining details are included with the Colour Key.

3   Remove the guidelines and steam press the worked piece flat after placing it face-down on a clean surface. If you are not using a steam iron, place a damp cloth over the wrong side of the evenweave before pressing it.

MAKING THE HEART:
1   With the design lying face-up on top, pin all three pieces of fabric together about 2" from each edge.

2   Fold the ribbon in half to form a loop, and catch the ends together with a stitch. Place the loop between the two pieces of plain white fabric so that its end lies behind the gold heart on the design. Hold it in position with a pin.

3   Baste through all three layers, ⅛" away from the edge of the design, making sure that you catch the ribbon in place. Leave an opening of about 2" along one side so that you can pad out the heart with wadding.

4   Working just outside the basting stitches, hand or machine-stitch around the design, and then remove both the basting and the pins. (Remember to leave your opening!)

5   Trim around the heart with pinking shears, ⅜" from your stitching line. Be careful not to cut through the ribbon – you will need to pink both in front and behind it.

6   Pad the heart with wadding between the two pieces of plain fabric, and finish by slipstitching your opening closed along the stitching line.

COLOUR KEY					
⊟	368	Pale Forest Green	❷	680	Dark Gold
1	519	Turquoise Blue	Ⅱ		Gold Metallic Thread

OUTLINING

— Use 2 strands of 680 Dark Gold for the beaks

Handbag Mirror

The humblest of plants has a
romance and mystery of its own –
see how common bindweed serves
as a dramatic centrepiece for this
striking design

YOU WILL NEED:
to make one mirror, 2⅝" round

To stitch the design:
7" x 7" of white cotton aida (18 count)
1 x 8m skein of DMC stranded embroidery cotton in
   each of the 5 colours listed in the Colour Key
Size 26 tapestry needle
Coloured cotton for marking the guidelines

To assemble the mirror:
4" x 4" of medium-weight iron-on black interfacing
White card
Pins
Scissors
2⅝" round handbag mirror. For suppliers see p.122

STITCHING THE DESIGN:
1 Tack guidelines with coloured cotton to mark the
   centre of the aida before positioning it on your hoop
   or frame. This design will fit into a 5" embroidery
   hoop.
2 Join the arrows on the chart to find the centre of the
   design, and stitch the piece using 2 strands of cotton
   for all cross stitches. There is no outlining on this
   design.
3 Remove the guidelines and steam press the worked
   piece flat after placing it face-down on a clean surface.
   If you are not using a steam iron, place a damp cloth
   over the wrong side of the aida before pressing it.

ASSEMBLING THE MIRROR:
1 With the design face-down, iron the interfacing on to
   the wrong side of the aida, making sure that you cover
   all the stitching. The interfacing adds stability to the
   fabric and also prevents stitches from fraying when
   you trim the design to fit the mirror.
2 Make a template of your mirror by placing the rim
   face-up on white card and drawing around the inside
   edge of the rim. If you draw around the outside, the
   design will not fit the mirror without distorting.
3 Cut out the template and pin it securely on top of
   your design so that the same amount of stitching
   shows on all sides.
4 Trim around the template as carefully as you can.
5 Finish assembling the mirror by following the
   supplier's instructions.

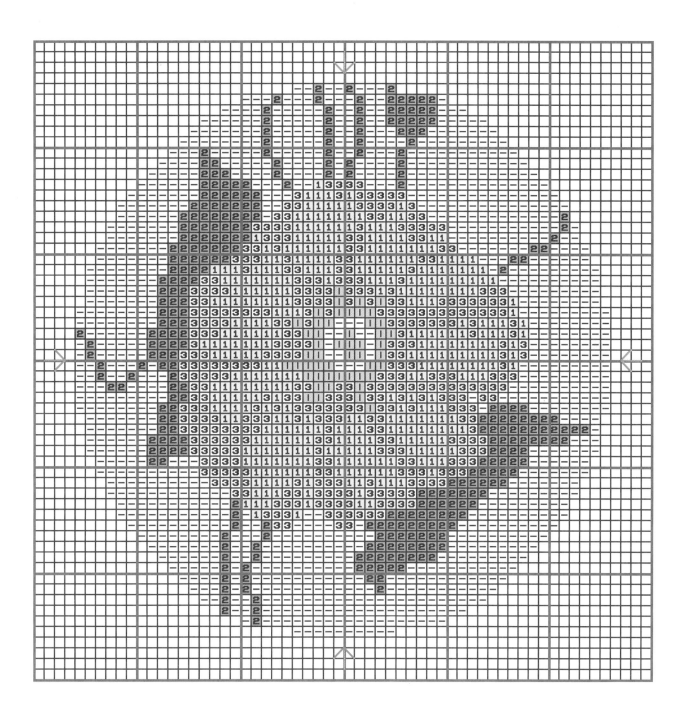

COLOUR KEY					
3		BLANC	I	743	Yellow
−	310	Black	1	800	Glazed Blue
2	703	Brilliant Green			

Lavender Sachet

A complete alphabet accompanies this old favourite – personalizing this delicate piece will transform it into a very special gift indeed

YOU WILL NEED:

to make one sachet, finished size 4½" x 3¼"approx

To stitch the design:

8" x 6¾" of white evenweave cotton (26 threads to the inch)

1 x 8m skein of DMC stranded embroidery cotton in each of the 6 colours listed in the Colour Key

Size 24 tapestry needle

2 lengths of different coloured cotton for marking guidelines

To make the sachet:

5½" x 4¼" of fine white cotton fabric (eg cotton lawn)

36" of white lace, 1" wide approx *(this will be gathered)*

White sewing cotton

Sharp sewing needle

Pins

Scissors

For the padding:

2 pieces of plain white cotton lawn fabric, both 5½" x 4¼"

Wadding

Lavender

STITCHING THE DESIGN:

1   To ensure that the motifs are worked in the correct position, you will need to mark guidelines on your fabric showing the perimeter of your working area. To do this, measure in 1¾" from each edge of the evenweave, and tack guidelines in coloured cotton [Colour A] along the nearest threads. You will have a rectangle of 4½" x 3¼" in the centre of the fabric.

2   To mark guidelines indicating the centres of the motifs, measure in 2¾" from the bottom and the two sides of the evenweave, and tack guidelines in a different coloured cotton [Colour B] along the nearest threads. Measure 2⅝" from the top and tack a fourth guideline in the same colour. The points where the guidelines in Colour B cross at top left and bottom right are the points where your stitching should be centred.

3   Join the arrows on the chart to find the centre of the floral motif, and then stitch it in the bottom right-hand corner of the fabric using 2 strands of cotton for all cross stitches. There is no outlining on this motif.

4   To position your initial correctly, plot it in the empty box on the chart, with the left-hand edge of the letter touching the left-hand edge of the box. The letters vary in width, and you may well find that the central vertical guideline (shown by an arrow on the chart) does not pass through the centre of your letter. Do not be concerned about this, but stitch the letter as you have plotted it using 2 strands of cotton.

3   Remove the guidelines in Colour B only and steam press the worked piece flat after placing it face-down on a clean surface. If you are not using a steam iron, place a damp cloth over the wrong side of the evenweave before pressing it.

MAKING THE SACHET:

1   Trim the evenweave to 5½" x 4¼", taking care that the working area remains centrally positioned.

2   Join the cut ends of the lace together with a small seam, and gather the lace until it fits neatly around the working area. Place the lace on the right side of the evenweave, with its straight-edge lying just outside the guidelines. Baste the lace into position and then fix it into place by hand-stitching. Remove the lace basting.

3   Place the evenweave (with lace attached) face-down on top of the backing material so that the right sides are together. Following the guidelines, pin a seamline joining the fabrics around the edge of the working area, leaving an opening of about 2" along the bottom. Remove the guidelines.

4   Working just outside the pins, hand or machine-stitch the seam. Trim the seam allowance to ½" and remove the pins.

5   Turn the fabrics right side out and insert the padding (see below) into the sachet through the opening. Slipstitch the opening closed along the seamline.

6   **To make the padding:**

a)   Place the two pieces of cotton lawn together and stitch a seam ½" from every side, leaving a 2" opening along one side to insert the filling. Trim the seam allowance to ¼" and turn the fabric right side out.

b)   Fill the pad with wadding and lavender to your required thickness and slipstitch the opening closed.

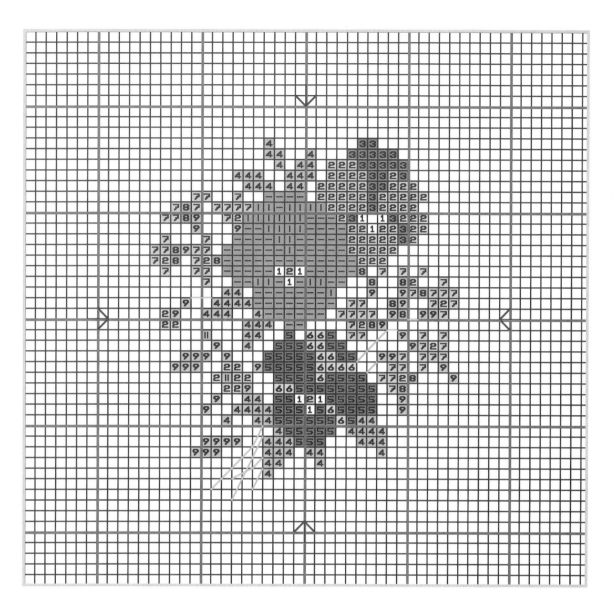

COLOUR KEY

1	310	Black	2	725	Yellow
5	333	Deep Periwinkle Blue	III	782	Burnished Gold
6	341	China Blue	3	783	Old Gold
8	604	Rose Pink	9	966	Pale Laurel
7	605	Pale Rose	4	988	Leaf Green
–	718	Raspberry	II	3608	Cyclamen Pink

OUTLINING

Use 2 strands of 966 Pale Laurel for the stems

Use 2 strands of 988 Leaf Green for the stems

Kitten
Picture

❧

*V*ery small, and very naughty,
Mitten is usually to be found
sheltering under the hedge, waiting for
the birds to come along…

YOU WILL NEED:

Design size 2" x 1⅞" approx

To stitch the design:

5" x 5" of white cotton aida (14 count)

1 x 8m skein of DMC stranded embroidery cotton in each of the 10 colours listed in the Colour Key and Outlining

Size 24 tapestry needle

Coloured cotton for marking the guidelines

To mount the embroidery:

3¼" x 3⅛" of white mounting board

Pins

Double-sided tape (½" wide)

Masking tape (1" wide)

STITCHING THE DESIGN

1 Tack guidelines with coloured cotton to mark the centre of the aida before positioning it on your hoop or frame. This design will fit into a 4" hoop.
2 Join the arrows on the chart to find the centre of the design, and stitch the piece using 2 strands of cotton for all cross stitches. Outlining details are included with the Colour Key.
3 Do not remove the guidelines, but steam press the worked piece flat after placing it face-down on a clean surface. If you are not using a steam iron, place a damp cloth over the wrong side of the aida before pressing it.

MOUNTING THE EMBROIDERY:

1 Trim the aida to 4¼" x 4⅛", ensuring that the design remains centrally positioned.
2 With the design face-down, place the mounting board centrally over the aida. To do this, mark the mid-point on all four sides of the card, and align these points with the guidelines on your fabric.
3 Place a pin into the thickness of the board at each of these four points, joining the aida and the board together. Turn the board over so that you can see the embroidery.
4 Starting at the top of the design, place pins at regular intervals into the thickness of the board to stretch the aida. Work from the mid-point to each side, and keep the fabric as flat and square as you can. This is done by keeping the thread of aida nearest to the edge as straight as possible, and pulling the fabric so that it lies flat but does not distort.
5 Repeat the process around the other three sides of the design *(working top-side-bottom-side)*, but on these sides work from a pinned corner to the opposite corner. You may well find that your central pins will need to be moved as the embroidery is stretched.
6 When you have pinned all four sides, make any necessary adjustments, remove the guidelines, and place the design face-down.
7 Cut a strip of double-sided tape 3¼" long, and lay it along the top edge of the board. Fold the aida over so that it is held securely by the tape and then repeat the process around the other three edges *(working top-bottom-side-side)*, with the tape at the two sides being 3⅛" long. The corners will have an extra thickness, but try to keep them as flat as you can.
8 Cover the raw edges of the fabric with strips of masking tape and remove all pins. The design will be shown to best effect in a small picture mount that slightly overlaps the stitches around all four sides.

This method of mounting embroidery is very suitable for small designs such as those in this book. If you wish to mount large designs, or embroideries worked on heavy-weight fabrics, we recommend that the work is done by a professional stretcher and framer who will probably use lacing thread.

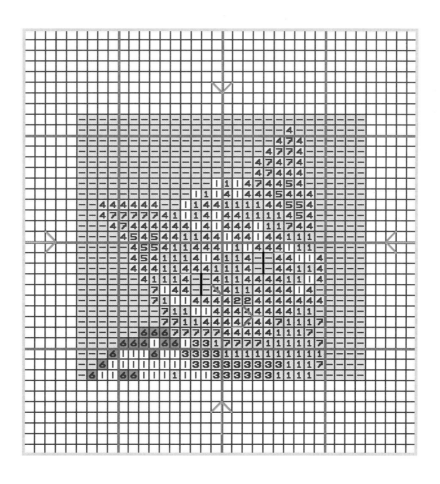

COLOUR KEY					
②	316	Strawberry	⑤	778	Light Strawberry
⑥	318	Grey	⊟	993	Jade
①	613	Stone	③	3012	Dark Stone
Ⅱ	645	Mid Grey	⑦	3047	Fawn
④	746	Pale Toffee			

OUTLINING

━━━ Use 2 strands of 535 Dark Grey for the pupils of the eyes

━━━ Use 1 strand of 535 Dark Grey for all other outlining

Anniversary Rose Card

The rose is a universal symbol of romance – you can send this card to remind someone of your love

YOU WILL NEED:

to make one card, with a design size 3" x 2" approx

To stitch the design:

7" x 6" of white cotton aida (14 count)

1 x 8m skein of DMC stranded embroidery cotton in each of the 6 colours listed in the Colour Key

Size 24 tapestry needle

Coloured cotton for marking the guidelines

To assemble the card:

7" x 6" of medium-weight iron-on white interfacing

Double-sided tape (½" wide)

Three-leaved card mount with aperture 4" x 3" approx

Scissors

STITCHING THE DESIGN:

1   Tack guidelines with coloured cotton to mark the centre of the aida before positioning it on your hoop or frame. This design will fit into a 6" embroidery hoop.

2   Join the arrows on the chart to find the centre of the design, and stitch the piece using 2 strands of cotton for all cross stitches. There is no outlining on this design.

3   Remove the guidelines and steam press the worked piece flat after placing it face-down on a clean surface. If you are not using a steam iron, place a damp cloth over the wrong side of the aida before pressing it.

ASSEMBLING THE CARD:

1   After pressing your worked piece, leave it face-down and iron on the interfacing to provide necessary stiffening.

2   Place the aperture of the card over the design, and, if necessary, trim the stiffened aida to size. Keep the design centrally-positioned, and cut the fabric so that it overlaps the aperture by at least ¾" on each side.

3   Put strips of double-sided tape around the inside of the card, near to each edge of the aperture, and then position the taped side of the card over the design and press it down on to the fabric. Do not press too firmly until you are sure that your design is in the right place.

4   Lay the design face-down, with the bottom of the design nearest to you, and fix strips of double-sided tape on the left-hand leaf of the card. Press this tape firmly down on to the central leaf to hide the aida.

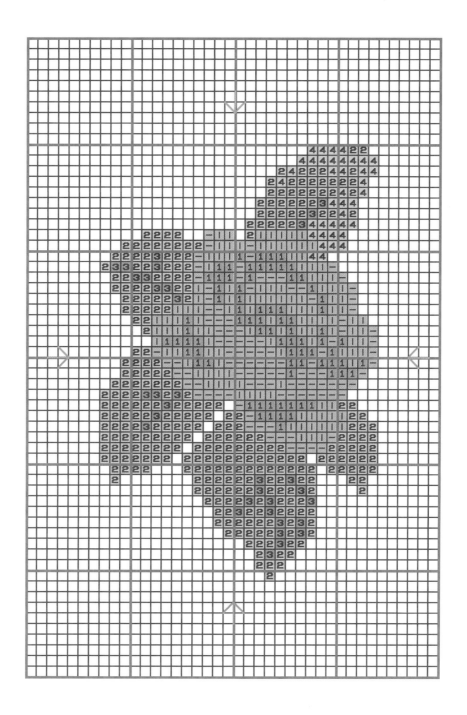

COLOUR KEY					
3	562	Dark Laurel Green	1	3705	Dark Coral Rose
2	563	Laurel Green	I	3706	Coral Rose
4	564	Pale Laurel Green	–	3708	Pale Coral Rose

Potpourri Sachet

Keep one of these small bags in a
drawer of your dressing-table to make
everything sweet-smelling – or, with its
delicate lace trimming, it would be
a wonderful gift

YOU WILL NEED:

to make one sachet, finished size (including lace trim)
7½" x 4½" approx

To stitch the design:

9" x 6½" of white evenweave cotton (26 threads to the inch)

1 x 8m skein of DMC stranded embroidery cotton in each of the 12 colours listed in the Colour Key

Size 24 tapestry needle

Coloured cotton for marking the guidelines

To make the sachet:

Another 9" x 6½" piece of white evenweave cotton (26 threads to the inch)

White sewing cotton

Sharp sewing needle

12" white lace trimming (½" wide)

About 24" of narrow double-sided white satin ribbon

Pins

Scissors

Potpourri to half-fill the sachet

STITCHING THE DESIGN:

1 Mark the vertical guideline by folding the short side of the fabric in half and following the central thread as normal.

2 To mark the horizontal guideline, measure up 2¼" from the bottom of the evenweave and follow the thread nearest to this point. You will see that the design is largely stitched in the bottom half of the fabric, as the point where your guidelines cross remains the point where the centre of the design should be positioned.

3 If you fix this design to a hoop take particular care not to mark the fabric. It may be better to use a small tapestry frame.

4 Join the arrows on the chart to find the centre of the design, and stitch the piece using 2 strands of cotton for all cross stitches. Outlining details are included with the Colour Key.

5 Remove the guidelines and steam press the worked piece flat after placing it face-down on a clean surface. If you are not using a steam iron, place a damp cloth over the wrong side of the fabric before pressing it.

MAKING THE SACHET:

1 Turn the design face-up and lay the second piece of fabric on top of it.

2 Join the pieces of fabric together by basting stitches along the sides and bottom, taking about a 1" seam from the edge. Hand or machine-stitch along the seam and remove the basting stitches.

3 Trim the seam allowances to about ½" wide, and turn the sachet right side out. Take care that the seams lie as flat as possible inside the sachet.

4 Turn over 1" of fabric into the top of the sachet and hold it in place by basting stitches near to the new top edge.

5 Measure the lace trimming against the top of the sachet and pin the two short edges of the lace together to mark the exact length that you need.

6 Make a small seam at the pin and trim off excess lace to within about ¼" before folding the two ends backwards and pressing the seam open.

7 Turn the seam inside and pin the trimming to the top of the sachet, along the inside edge. Baste stitches to hold it in place and then remove the pins.

8 Working from the right side of the fabric, hand or machine-stitch the trimming in place, sewing close to the top edge. Remove all basting.

9 Half-fill the sachet with potpourri and tie the ribbon twice around the sachet just above the potpourri, finishing with a bow in front.

COLOUR KEY					
▣	553	Violet	4	776	Strawberry Pink
⊟	554	Pale Violet	3	3345	Dark Green
1	727	Spring Yellow	2	3347	Green

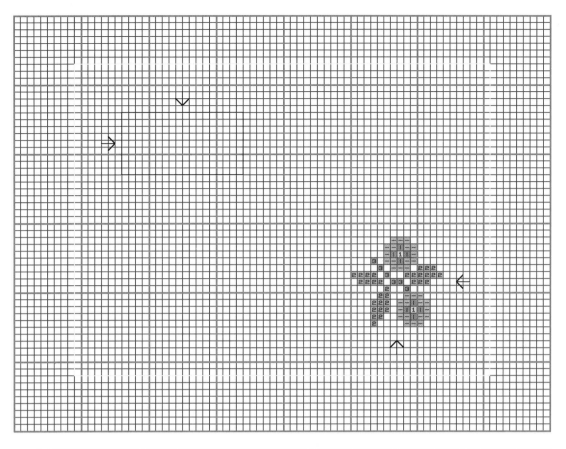

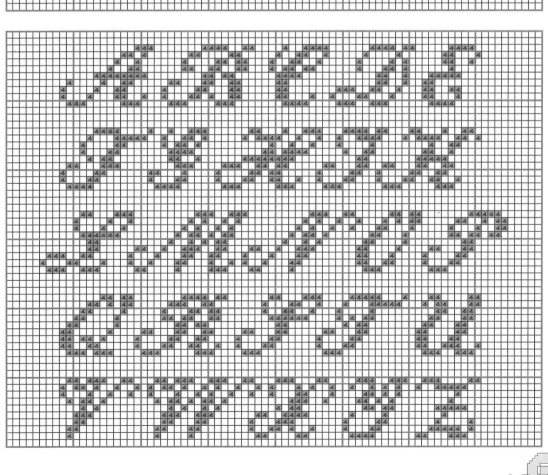

Squirrel Purse

Each year the squirrels strip all the hazelnuts from our tree and bury them in the grass for winter food. You can squirrel away your change in this canvas purse that they have inspired

YOU WILL NEED:

to make one purse, finished size 4" x 3" approx

To stitch the design:

2 pieces of white single thread interlock canvas (18 holes to the inch) cut to 6" x 6"

1 x 8m skein of DMC stranded embroidery cotton in each of the colours listed in the Colour Key, except shade 310 Black

6 x 8m skeins of DMC stranded embroidery cotton, shade 310 Black

Size 24 tapestry needle

Coloured cotton for marking the guidelines

To make the purse:

2 pieces of medium-weight iron-on black interfacing cut to 6" x 6"

Double-sided tape (½" wide)

4" Black zip

Black sewing cotton

Sharp sewing needle

Scissors

STITCHING THE DESIGN:

1 Take one piece of canvas, and tack guidelines with coloured cotton to mark the centre. You should find that the canvas is stiff enough to work it in your hand, but you may wish to fix it to a small tapestry frame. Do not use an embroidery hoop!

2 Join the arrows on the chart to find the centre of the design, and stitch the piece using 3 strands of cotton for all cross stitches. Outlining details are included with the Colour Key.

3 Stitch each cross stitch over one intersection of canvas only (see The Basics of Cross Stitch p.14)

4 To stitch the back of the purse, find the centre of the second piece of canvas and work a rectangle of cross stitches measuring 75 stitches by 56 stitches in 310 Black.

5 Remove the guidelines from both pieces of canvas, and gently ease them flat and square by pulling at each corner. You should not use steam on canvas unless it has been properly 'blocked' by a professional stretcher.

MAKING THE PURSE:

1 Take the front of the purse. Measure ½" away from the stitching on all four sides and trim the canvas to size.

2 Turn the design face-down, and place a strip of double-sided tape along the ½" turnings at both the top and bottom of the canvas. Fold the turnings down behind the stitching, making sure that the tape holds securely. Tape down the turnings at the sides in the same way.

3 Place one piece of interfacing over the canvas, trim it to size, and then iron it on to the wrong side of the canvas. (Remember that you must not use steam near canvas.)

4 Repeat steps 1–3 above with the back of the purse.

5 Turn the front of the purse face-down and position the zip, also right side down, along the top edge, basting stitches ⅛" from the top. Hand or machine-stitch the zip in place, working close to the basting stitches, and remove the basting.

6 Put the two pieces of canvas right sides together and, with the back of the purse on top, fix the zip in place on the second piece of canvas.

7 If there are any ends of the zip overlapping the canvas at the sides, fold them to the inside of the purse and catch them with small stitches.

8 Turn the purse right sides out and oversew the front and back sections together using 3 strands of 310 Black.

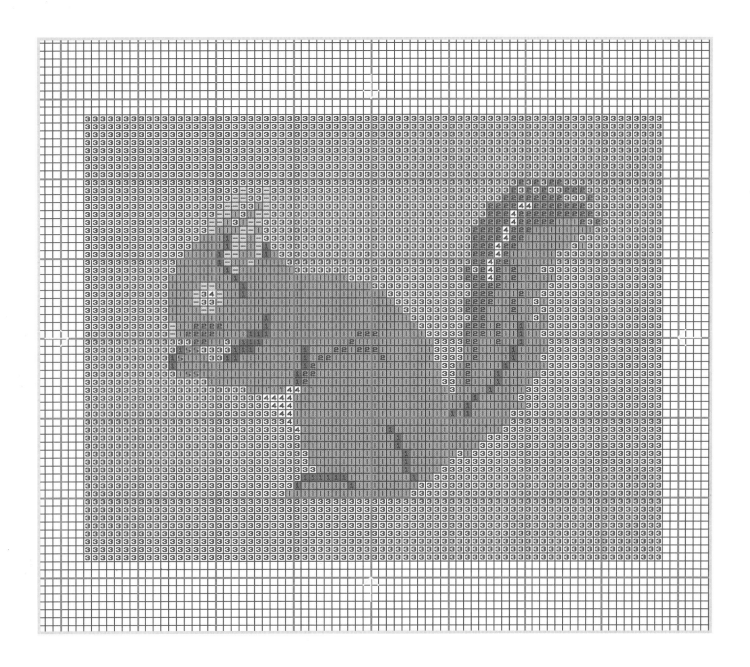

COLOUR KEY

4		BLANC	5	701	Bright Green
1	301	Chestnut	−	945	Bronze Flesh
3	310	Black	I	976	Russet Brown
2	402	Pale Chestnut			

OUTLINING

──── Use 1 strand of 310 Black around the eye

Poinsettia Picture

The vivid petals of this Christmas favourite make a wonderful subject for a cross stitch picture that can be enjoyed throughout the year

YOU WILL NEED:
Design size 2¾" x 2¾" approx

To stitch the design:
9" x 9" of white cotton aida (18 count)

1 x 8m skein of DMC stranded embroidery cotton in each of the 9 colours listed in the Colour Key and Outlining

Size 26 tapestry needle

Coloured cotton for marking the guidelines

To mount the embroidery:
5" x 5" of white mounting board

Pins

Double-sided tape (½" wide)

Masking tape (1" wide)

STITCHING THE DESIGN:
1 Tack guidelines with coloured cotton to mark the centre of the aida before positioning it on your hoop or frame. This design will fit into a 6" embroidery hoop.

2 Join the arrows on the chart to find the centre of the design, and stitch the piece using 2 strands of cotton for all cross stitches. Outlining details are included with the Colour Key.

3 Do not remove the guidelines, but steam press the worked piece flat after placing it face-down on a clean surface. If you are not using a steam iron, place a damp cloth over the wrong side of the aida before pressing it.

MOUNTING THE EMBROIDERY:
1 Trim the aida to 7" x 7", ensuring that the design remains centrally positioned

2 With the design face-down, place the mounting board centrally over the aida. To do this, mark the mid-point on all four sides of the card, and align these points with the guidelines on your fabric.

3 Place a pin into the thickness of the board at each of these four points, joining the aida and the board together. Turn the board over so that you can see the embroidery.

4 Starting at the top of the design, place pins at regular intervals into the thickness of the board to stretch the aida. Work from the mid-point to each side, and keep the fabric as flat and square as you can. This is done by keeping the thread of aida nearest to the edge as straight as possible, and pulling the fabric so that it lies flat but does not distort.

5 Repeat the process around the other three sides of the design (working top-side-bottom-side), but on these sides work from a pinned corner to the opposite corner. You may well find that your central pins will need to be moved as the embroidery is stretched.

6 When you have pinned all four sides, make any necessary adjustments, remove the guidelines, and place the design face-down.

7 Cut a strip of double-sided tape 5" long, and lay it along the top edge of the board. Fold the aida over so that it is held securely by the tape and then repeat the process around the other three sides (working top-bottom-side-side). The corners will have an extra thickness, but try to keep them as flat as you can.

8 Cover the raw edges of the fabric with strips of masking tape and remove all pins.

This method of mounting embroidery is very suitable for small designs such as those in this book. If you wish to mount large designs, or embroideries worked on heavy-weight fabrics, we recommend that the work is done by a professional stretcher and framer who will probably use lacing thread.

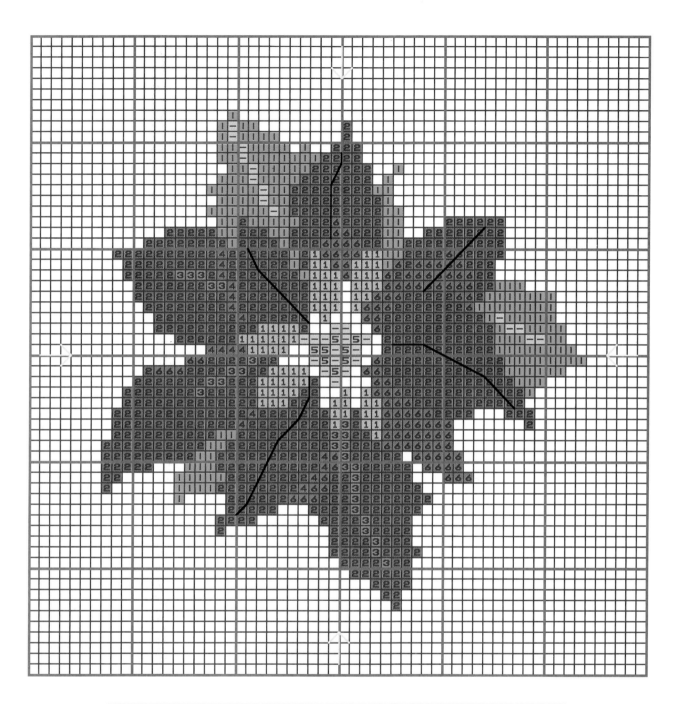

<table>
<tr><th colspan="6" style="text-align:center">COLOUR KEY</th></tr>
</table>

5	307	Buttercup Yellow	4	817	Scarlet
6	349	Bright Flame Red	−	966	Pale Laurel
1	352	Coral	I	988	Leaf Green
2	606	Flame Red	3	989	Mid Green

OUTLINING

— Use 1 strand of 304 Deep Red for the veins in the flower petals

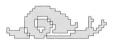

Trinket Box

When the rain is falling and the fog descends, this little box will remind you of those long, hot summer days when the sun beats down on golden cornfields speckled with poppies

YOU WILL NEED:
to make one box, 3½" round

To stitch the design:
8" x 8" of cream cotton aida (14 count)
1 x 8m skein of DMC stranded embroidery cotton in each of the 8 colours listed in the Colour Key and Outlining
Size 24 tapestry needle
Coloured cotton for marking the guidelines

To assemble the lid of the bowl:
6" x 6" of medium-weight iron-on white interfacing
Pencil
Scissors
3½" round frosted glass bowl. For suppliers see p.122

STITCHING THE DESIGN:
1 Tack guidelines with coloured cotton to mark the centre of the aida before positioning it on your hoop or frame. This design will fit into a 6" embroidery hoop.
2 Join the arrows on the chart to find the centre of the design, and stitch the piece using 2 strands of cotton for all cross stitches. Outlining details are included with the Colour Key.
3 Remove the guidelines and steam press the worked piece flat after placing it face-down on a clean surface. If you are not using a steam iron, place a damp cloth over the wrong side of the aida before pressing it.

ASSEMBLING THE LID OF THE BOX:
1 With the design face-down, iron the interfacing on to the wrong side of the aida, making sure that you cover all the stitching. The interfacing adds stability to the fabric and also prevents it from fraying when you trim the design to fit the lid.
2 Use the acetate provided as a template to ensure that the design is trimmed to the correct size. Position the acetate centrally over your stitching so that the design shows to best advantage and then mark a line around it with a pencil.
3 Cut around the inside edge of the pencil line as carefully as you can so that the design fits without distortion.
4 Finish assembling the lid by following the supplier's instructions.

COLOUR KEY					
1	310	Black	2	702	Emerald Green
3	564	Pale Laurel Green	4	725	Corn Yellow
−	606	Bright Red	5	989	Mid Green
I	608	Orange Flame			

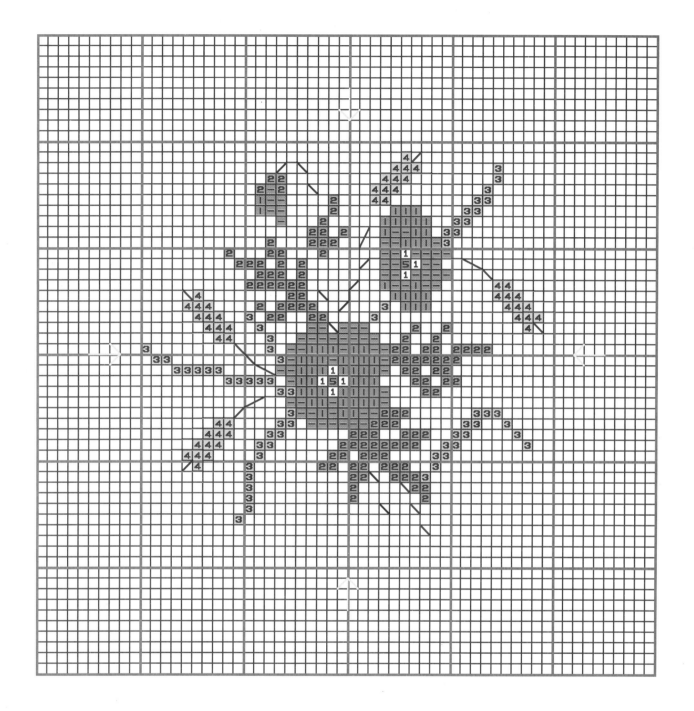

OUTLINING

━━ Use 2 strands of 702 Emerald Green for poppy stems

━━ Use 2 strands of 564 Pale Laurel Green for the poppy stem

━━ Use 1 strand of 782 Burnished Gold to outline the corn and its stems

Cosmetics Bag

❦

*T*his simple bag has been specially created to hold your essential make-up – with its cheerful design worked on bright red fabric it will cheer up the ugliest of days!

YOU WILL NEED:

to make one bag, finished size 6½" x 4½" approx

To stitch the design:

12¾" x 7½" of red cotton aida (14 count)

1 x 8m skein of DMC stranded embroidery cotton in each of the 3 colours listed in the Colour Key

Size 24 tapestry needle

Coloured cotton for marking the guidelines

To make the bag:

12¾" x 7½" of red lining material

12¾" x 7½" of iron-on white quilted interfacing

1½ yds of red bias binding (⅝" wide)

Red sewing cotton to match your binding

Sharp sewing needle

Pins

Scissors

STITCHING THE DESIGN:

1   Mark the vertical guideline by folding the short side of the fabric in half and following the central thread as normal.

2   To mark the horizontal guideline, count 30 squares from the bottom of the aida and follow the thread between the 30th and 31st squares. The positioning of the design is especially critical in this project, and this method ensures correct placement.

3   You will see that the design is stitched towards the bottom of the fabric. The point where your guidelines cross remains the point where the centre of the design should be positioned.

4   It is better to use a small tapestry frame for this design because the aida is too large to fit comfortably into an embroidery hoop.

5   Join the arrows on the chart to find the centre of the design, and stitch the piece using 2 strands of cotton for all cross stitches. There is no outlining on this design.

6   Remove the guidelines and steam press the worked piece flat after placing it face-down on a clean surface. If you are not using a steam iron, place a damp cloth over the wrong side of the fabric before pressing it.

MAKING THE BAG:

1   Iron the interfacing on to the lining material.

2   Turn the aida face-down, and place the other fabrics on top of it, with the lining material uppermost. Join the pieces of fabric together with pins, taking a ½" seam from each edge. Hand or machine-stitch along the seams and remove the pins.

3   Turn the design face-up, and place pins at each side of the aida on the thread marking the upper limit of the design.

4   With the design face-up and at the bottom, trim the seam allowance to ¼" along the top edge only and attach bias binding (see 9 below) along that edge.

5   Place the aida face-down and turn it so that the design now lies at the top.

6   To make the pocket of the bag, fold the bound edge up to the pins which mark the limit of your stitching. Baste stitches down each side of the pocket, following the existing seamlines, and then hand or machine-stitch once again along each seam and remove the basting stitches and pins.

7   Trim all seam allowances to ¼", and attach bias binding around the sides and top of the bag. On this occasion, you should fold over the cut ends of the binding by about ¼" to prevent them fraying, and neaten them off finally by oversewing.

8   Fold the top of the bag over so that the design shows in front.

9   **To attach bias binding:**

a) Open out the turning on one edge of the binding, and pin it in position on the right side of the fabric, matching the edge of the binding to the raw edges of the seam allowance(s). Secure the binding by hand or machine-stitching along the seamline(s) and remove the pins.

b) Fold the binding over the raw edges on to the wrong side of the fabric, and hold it in position with pins or basting stitches before neatly hemming it to finish. Make sure that you remove all pins and basting stitches.

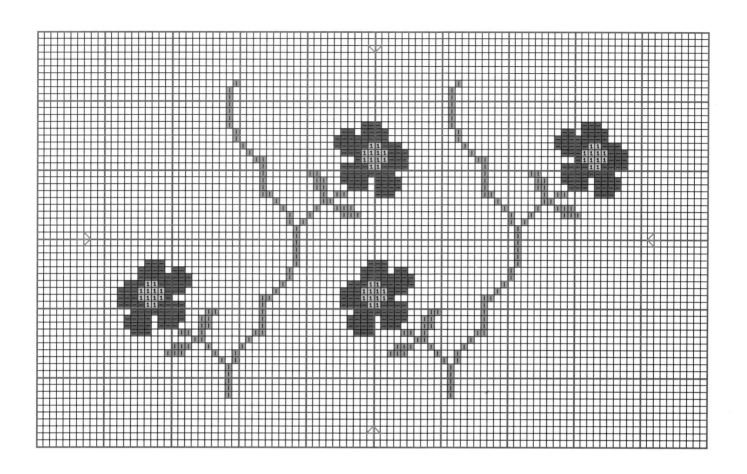

<table>
<tr><th colspan="6" align="center">C O L O U R   K E Y</th></tr>
</table>

■	792	Deep Blue	Ⅱ	992	Jade Green
1	972	Bright Yellow			

Victorian Handkerchief Sachet

Antique linen and lace trimming combine to recreate a simple, but treasured, possession from times past – a keepsake once to be found on every lady's dressing-table

YOU WILL NEED:
to make one sachet, finished size 7½" x 7½" approx

To stitch the design:
14" x 14" of antique evenweave linen (28 threads to the inch)
1 x 8m skein of DMC stranded embroidery cotton in each of the 5 colours listed in the Colour Key and Outlining
Size 26 tapestry needle
2 lengths of different coloured cotton for marking guide-lines

To make the sachet:
11¾" x 11¾" of plain white cotton lining
48" of white lace trimming, ¾" wide approx
DMC BLANC stranded embroidery cotton
Button, ⅜" wide approx
White sewing cotton
Sharp sewing needle
Pins
Scissors

STITCHING THE DESIGN:
1 To ensure that the designs are worked in the correct position, you will need to mark guidelines on your linen showing the perimeter of your working area. To do this, measure in 1⅝" from each edge of the linen, and tack guidelines in coloured cotton [Colour A] along the nearest threads. You will have a square of 10¾" x 10¾" in the centre of the fabric.
2 To mark guidelines showing the centres of the designs, measure in 3¼" from each edge of the linen, and tack guidelines in a different coloured cotton [Colour B] along the nearest threads. You will now also have an inner square of 7½" x 7½". The points where the guidelines in Colour B cross are the points where your stitching should be centred.
3 Join the arrows on the chart to find the centre of the design, and then stitch it in each corner of the linen using 2 strands of cotton for all cross stitches. Outlining details are included with the Colour Key.
4 To make sure that you stitch the design correctly in each corner, you may find it easier to turn the fabric around so that you can work each corner in the same way.
5 Remove the guidelines in Colour B only and steam press the worked piece flat after placing it face-down on a clean surface. If you are not using a steam iron, place a damp cloth over the wrong side of the linen before pressing it.

MAKING THE SACHET:
1 Trim the linen to 11¾" x 11¾", taking care that the working area remains centrally positioned.
2 Following the guidelines all the way around, fold over ½" of linen on to the wrong side and baste it close to the edge. Remove the coloured guidelines and trim the turning near to the basting.
3 Take the cotton lining and fold over ½" around all sides. Baste the turning close to the edge, and trim it near to your stitching.
4 Place the linen and its lining wrong sides together, and pin them all around. Oversew along the edges with white sewing cotton so that the two pieces of fabric are securely joined and remove all pins and basting.
5 Attach lace trimming (see 8 below) along all four sides.
6 Turn the linen face-down, and bring the four corners to the centre to form the sachet.
7 Keeping the corners in position with small weights, sew the button on to one of the corners, and, using all 6 strands of the BLANC stranded embroidery cotton, fix loops on each of the other three corners, just large enough for the button to pass through comfortably.

8 To attach lace trimming:
a) Pin the trimming to the right side of your fabric so that half of its width will show. Cut off any excess length, and hem the lace into position removing the pins as you go. You will need to make small mitres at each corner so that they lie as neatly as possible.
b) Turn the fabric over and fold the second half of the trimming on to the wrong side, fixing it into position in the same way.

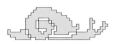

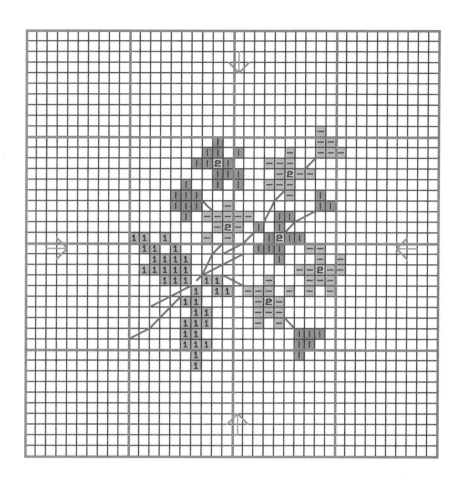

COLOUR KEY					
▣	553	Violet	▯	701	Bright Green
▬	603	Deep Pink	▨	744	Gorse Yellow

OUTLINING

▬ Use 1 strand of 699 Dark Bright Green for the stems

This same design is stitched in each of the four corners of the sachet

Rambling Rose Spectacle Case

Easy to stitch and very practical, this decorative canvas case will provide genuine protection for your spectacles and sunglasses

YOU WILL NEED:

to make one case, finished size 6" x 3" approx

To stitch the design:

2 pieces of white single thread interlock canvas (18 holes to the inch) cut to 9" x 6"

1 x 8m skein of DMC stranded embroidery cotton in each of the colours listed in the Colour Key, except shade 327 Mauve

6 x 8m skeins of DMC stranded embroidery cotton, shade 327 Mauve

Size 24 tapestry needle

Coloured cotton for marking the guidelines

To make the case:

2 pieces of white felt cut to 9" x 6"

Double-sided tape (½" wide)

Scissors

STITCHING THE DESIGN:

1 Take one piece of canvas, and tack guidelines with coloured cotton to mark the centre. You should find that the canvas is stiff enough to work it in your hand, but you may wish to fix it to a small tapestry frame. Do not use an embroidery hoop!

2 Join the arrows on the chart to find the centre of the design, and stitch the piece using 3 strands of cotton for all cross stitches. There is no outlining on this design.

3 Stitch each cross stitch over one intersection of canvas only (see The Basics of Cross Stitch p.14).

4 Work the design in the same way on the second piece of canvas. Label the pieces 'front' and 'back'.

5 Remove the guidelines from both pieces of canvas, and gently ease them flat and square by pulling at each corner. You should not use steam on canvas unless it has been properly 'blocked' by a professional stretcher.

TO MAKE THE CASE:

1 Take the front of the case. Measure ½" away from the stitching on all four sides and trim the canvas to size.

2 Turn the design face-down, and place a strip of double-sided tape along the ½" turnings at both sides of the canvas. Fold the turnings down behind the stitching, making sure that the tape holds securely. Tape down the turnings at the top and bottom in the same way.

3 Place one piece of white felt over the canvas and trim it to size – it is important for the finished look of the case that the felt does not overlap the canvas at any point. Put the felt to one side.

4 With the design still face-down, fix further strips of double-sided tape very close to all the edges of the canvas and position the felt, pressing it by hand on to the tape.

5 Oversew the raw edge at the top of the design only using 3 strands of 327 Mauve, and taking care to catch the edge of the felt into your stitches. Do not oversew the other edges at this point.

6 Repeat steps 1–5 above with the back of the case.

7 Place the two canvas pieces with the designs right side out, and oversew the front and back of the case together around the sides and bottom using 3 strands of 327 Mauve.

COLOUR KEY					
1	319	Dark Green	5	966	Pale Laurel
7	327	Mauve	6	973	Bright Yellow
3	604	Rose Pink	I	988	Leaf Green
4	605	Pale Rose	−	989	Mid Green
2	921	Terracotta			

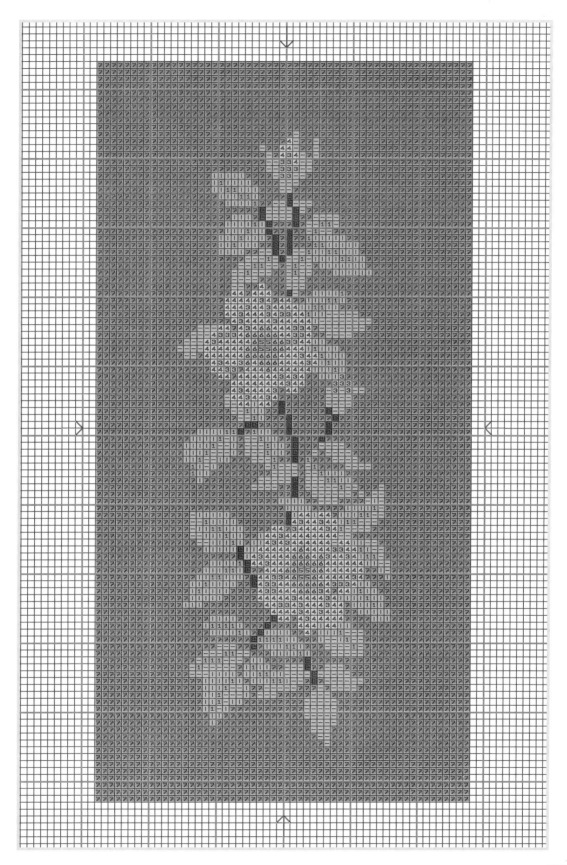

Herbal Pillow

After making this beautiful pillow, fill it with aromatic herbs and place it on your bed. It will help you to relax and sleep soundly every night

YOU WILL NEED:
to make one pillow, finished size 10" x 8" approx

To stitch the design:
12" x 10" of white evenweave cotton (26 threads to the inch)

1 x 8m skein of DMC stranded embroidery cotton in each of the 18 colours listed in the Colour Key and Outlining

Size 24 tapestry needle

Coloured cotton for marking the guidelines

To make the pillow:
11" x 9" of plain white cotton fabric (eg fine sheeting)

48" of double-sided white satin ribbon, $\frac{1}{8}$" (3mm) wide

Large-eyed tapestry needle or weaving needle

White sewing cotton

Sharp sewing needle

Pins

Scissors

For the cushion pad:
2 pieces of plain white cotton lawn fabric, both 11" x 9"

Wadding

Your chosen scented mixture

STITCHING THE DESIGN:
1 Tack guidelines with coloured cotton to mark the centre of the evenweave before positioning it on a small frame. This design is too large to fit comfortably in an embroidery hoop.

2 Join the arrows on the chart to find the centre of the design, and stitch the piece using 2 strands of cotton for all cross stitches. Outlining details are included with the Colour Key.

3 Remove the guidelines and steam press the worked piece flat after placing it face-down on a clean surface. If you are not using a steam iron, place a damp cloth over the wrong side of the cotton before pressing it.

MAKING THE PILLOW:
1 Turn the design face-up and trim the evenweave to 11" x 9", ensuring that the design remains centrally positioned.

2 Measure in 2" from every edge and carefully withdraw the two nearest threads from the evenweave. This creates the space for the ribbon to go through.

3 Cut 2 x 15" lengths and 2 x 13" lengths from the ribbon, and thread a 13" length through the large-eyed tapestry needle or weaving needle.

4 Place the needle in the space created by the withdrawn threads 2" from the left-hand side of the evenweave, and weave the ribbon across the fabric. Work under 5 threads to start, and then over 8 threads on the right side of the fabric, repeating this all the way across. You must be very careful not to distort the shape of the fabric by pulling the ribbon too firmly.

5 Weave ribbon across the remaining three sides in the same way.

6 Pin your backing fabric on top of the evenweave so that the right sides are together, and baste a seamline $\frac{1}{2}$" from each edge, making sure that you secure the ribbons in place. Leave an opening of about 6" along one side so that you can insert the cushion pad. Hand or machine-stitch along the seam and remove the basting stitches.

7 Trim the seam allowance to $\frac{1}{4}$". You may wish to oversew the raw edges of the allowance to prevent them fraying.

8 Turn the pillow right side out, keeping the seams as flat as possible, and insert the cushion pad (see 9 below). Slipstitch the opening closed along the seamline.

9 To make a cushion pad:
a) Place the two pieces of cotton lawn together and stitch a seam $\frac{1}{2}$" from every side, leaving a 5" opening along one side to insert the wadding. Trim the seam allowance to $\frac{1}{4}$" and turn the fabric right side out.

b) Fill the pad with wadding and the scented mixture to your required thickness and slipstitch the opening closed.

COLOUR KEY

◇		BLANC	1	742	Orange
I	211	Pale Lilac	⊠	832	Dark Mustard
6	367	Forest Green	∷	841	Dark Beige
5	368	Mid Forest Green	7	842	Beige
4	472	Pale Spring Green	=	963	Pale Pink
—	554	Violet	3	3345	Dark Green
9	725	Yellow	2	3347	Mid Green
8	727	Pale Yellow	III	3348	Moss Green

OUTLINING

— Use 2 strands of 3348 Moss Green for the violet stems
— Use 1 strand of 648 Stone Grey around the peony flowers
— Use 1 strand of 834 Golden Maize around the marigold flowers

Still Life

For the final project, something larger – a subject usually associated with painting for you to work in cross stitch. When you have successfully completed this, you will be able to tackle anything – good luck!

YOU WILL NEED:
Design size 5½" x 4¼" approx

To stitch the design:
12" x 10" of cream cotton aida (14 count)
1 x 8m skein of DMC stranded embroidery cotton in
    each of the 29 colours listed in the Colour Key
Size 24 tapestry needle
Coloured cotton for marking the guidelines

To mount the embroidery:
7½" x 6½" of white mounting board
Pins
Double-sided tape (1" wide)
Masking tape (1" wide)

STITCHING THE DESIGN:
1 Tack guidelines with coloured cotton to mark the
   centre of the aida before positioning it on your frame.
   This design does not fit comfortably into an embroidery hoop.
2 Join the arrows on the chart to find the centre of the
   design, and stitch the piece using 2 strands of cotton
   for all cross stitches. Outlining details are included
   with the Colour Key.
3 Do not remove the guidelines, but steam press the
   worked piece flat after placing it face-down on a clean
   surface. If you are not using a steam iron, place a
   damp cloth over the wrong side of the aida before
   pressing it.

MOUNTING THE EMBROIDERY:
1 Trim the aida to 9½" x 8½" ensuring that the design
   remains centrally positioned.
2 With the design face-down, place the mounting board
   centrally over the aida. To do this, mark the mid-
   point on all four sides of the card, and align these
   points with the guidelines on your fabric.
3 Place a pin into the thickness of the board at each of
   these four points, joining the aida and the board
   together. Turn the board over so that you can see the
   embroidery.
4 Starting at the top of the design, place pins at regular
   intervals into the thickness of the board to stretch the
   aida. Work from the mid-point to each side, and keep
   the fabric as flat and square as you can. This is done
   by keeping the thread of aida nearest to the edge as
   straight as possible, and pulling the fabric so that it
   lies flat but does not distort.
5 Repeat the process around the other three sides of the
   design *(working top-side-bottom-side)*, but on these
   sides work from a pinned corner to the opposite
   corner. You may well find that your central pins will
   need to be moved as the embroidery is stretched.
6 When you have pinned all four sides, make any necessary adjustments, remove the guidelines, and place the
   design face-down.
7 Cut a strip of double-sided tape 7½" long, and lay it
   on the board along one of the sides. Fold the aida
   over so that it is held securely by the tape and then
   repeat the process around the other three sides *(working side-side-top-bottom)*, with the tape at the top and
   bottom being 6½" long. The corners will have an
   extra thickness, but try to keep them as flat as you
   can.
8 Cover the raw edges of the fabric with strips of masking tape and remove all pins.

This method of mounting embroidery is very suitable for
small designs such as those in this book. If you wish to
mount large designs, or embroideries worked on heavy-
weight fabrics, we recommend that the work is done by a
professional stretcher and framer who will probably use
lacing thread.

OUTLINING

Use 1 strand of 828 Sky Blue around the yellow pansy
Use 2 strands of 310 Black in the centre of the red pansy
Use 2 strands of 580 Dark Moss Green for the flower stems

C O L O U R K E Y								
⊟		BLANC	◥	554	Pale Violet	◪	892	Deep Pink
⬠	210	Lilac	◿	580	Dark Moss Green	⑤	894	Mid Pink
◹	211	Pale Lilac	1	726	Yellow	⋀	900	Burnt Orange
◸	309	Carmine Rose	▮	740	Bright Orange	⊠	947	Orange Flame
3	310	Black	⊟	762	Light Grey	◈	977	Tangerine
2	413	Dark Grey	⁚⁚	775	Pale Sea Blue	9	3078	Pale Buttercup Yellow
Ⅲ	415	Grey	✚	781	Dark Gold	◩	3325	Sea Blue
8	471	Moss Green	⊕	783	Gold	◲	3347	Grass Green
⊠	552	Dark Violet	⓪	826	Kingfisher Blue	◿	3348	Pale Grass Green
◿	553	Violet	⊡	828	Sky Blue			

Suppliers

The basic items used in making up some of the projects in this book were kindly supplied by the following company, who will be pleased to forward goods by mail-order:

Framecraft Miniatures Ltd
372-376 Summer Lane
Hockley
Birmingham
B19 3QA
Great Britain
Telephone: 0121 212 0551

ADDRESSES OF FRAMECRAFT DISTRIBUTORS WORLDWIDE:

Anne Brinkley Designs Inc
761 Palmer Avenue
Holmdel
NJ 97733
USA
Telephone: 908 787 2011

Gay Bowles Sales Inc
PO Box 1060
Janesville
WI 53547
USA
Telephone: 608 754 9212

Danish Art Needlework
PO Box 442
Lethbridge
Alberta T1J 3Z1
Canada
Telephone: 403 327 9855

Ireland Needlecraft Pty Ltd
4,2-4 Keppel Drive
Hallam
Vic 3803
Australia
Telephone: 03702 3222

The Embroidery Shop
Greville-Parker
286 Queen Street
Masterton
New Zealand
Telephone: 6 377 1418

Eva Rosenstand a/s
Virumgardsvej 18
2830 Virum
Denmark
Telephone: 42 852 044

DMC
13 Rue de Pfastatt
68057 Mulhouse Cedex
France
Telephone: 89 32 44 44

Dollfus Mieg & Co
Viale Italia 84
1-20020 Lainate (MI)
Italy
Telephone: 2-93570427

Hannelore Kopp
Bayerischer Platz 7
1000 Berlin 30
Germany
Telephone: 853 9869

Sanyei Imports
PO Box 5
Hashima Shi
Gifu 501-62
Japan
Telephone: 0583 92 6532

For the name of your nearest stockist of Stranded Cotton, contact the following:

DMC

Great Britain

DMC Creative World Ltd
62 Pullman Road
Wigston
Leicester
LE8 2DY
Telephone: 0116 281 1040

Mainland Europe

DMC
13 Rue de Pfastatt
68057 Mulhouse Cedex
France
Telephone: 89 32 44 44

North America

The DMC Corporation
Port Kearney Bld.
#10 South Kearney
NJ 07032-0650
USA
Telephone: 201 589 0606

Australia and New Zealand

DMC Needlecraft Pty
PO Box 317
Earlswood 2206
NSW 2204
Australia
Telephone: 02599 3088

ANCHOR

Great Britain and Europe

Coats Patons Crafts
McMullen Road
Darlington
Co Durham
DL1 1YQ
Telephone: 01325 381010

North America

Coats & Clark
PO Box 27067
Dept CO1
Greenville
SC 29616
USA
Telephone: 803 234 0103

Australia and New Zealand

Coats Patons Crafts
Thistle Street
Launceston
Tasmania 7250
Australia
Telephone: 00344 4222

MADEIRA

Great Britain and Europe

Madeira Threads (UK) Ltd
Thirsk Industrial Park
York Road
Thirsk
N Yorks
YO7 3BX
Telephone: 01845 524880

North America

Madeira Marketing Ltd
600 East 9th Street
Michigan City
IN 46360
USA
Telephone: 219 873 1000

Australia and New Zealand:

Penguin Threads Pty Ltd
25-27 Izett Street
Prahran
Vic 3181
Australia
Telephone: 03529 4400

There are a large number of very good specialist needlecraft suppliers in Great Britain who will all be able to supply the items required to make up the projects in this book. If you have difficulty, however, the following will be pleased to help you:

Branches of **The John Lewis Partnership**
Branches of **New for Knitting**
Liberty, Regent Street, London, W1R 6AH
Creativity, 37/45 New Oxford Street, London WC1
The Voirrey Embroidery Centre, Brimstage Hall, Brimstage, Wirral, L63 6JA

Conversion Table

The table below lists the nearest equivalent colours in two other major ranges of Stranded Cotton.

It is impossible to give exact alternatives between different ranges, so the conversions are not perfect matches, but are in our opinion the closest substitutes available.

The table is intended as a guide only – if possible compare actual skeins before reaching a decision

DMC	Anchor	Madeira	DMC	Anchor	Madeira
Blanc	1	White	369	213	1701
209	109	0804	400	351	2305
210	108	0802	402	313	2307
211	342	0801	413	401	1713
301	349	2306	415	398	1802
304	47	0511	420	375	2105
307	289	0104	422	373	2102
309	42	0507	433	371	2008
310	403	Black	434	310	2009
316	969	0808	435	365	2010
317	235	1714	436	363	2011
318	399	1802	437	368	1910
319	246	1313	445	288	0103
327	101	0714	470	266	1502
333	119	0903	471	280	1501
341	117	0901	472	253	1414
349	13	0212	519	168	1105
351	10	0214	535	401	1809
352	9	0303	552	101	0713
367	262	1312	553	98	0712
368	261	1310	554	97	0711

DMC	Anchor	Madeira	DMC	Anchor	Madeira
562	210	1312	712	387	2101
563	204	1207	718	88	0707
564	203	1208	725	306	0113
580	268	1504	726	295	0109
597	168	1110	727	293	0110
598	928	1111	738	942	2013
603	62	0701	740	316	0203
604	55	0614	741	304	0201
605	50	0613	742	303	0114
606	335	0209	743	297	0113
608	333	0206	744	301	0112
610	905	2003	746	275	0101
611	898	2107	747	158	1104
612	832	2108	762	397	1804
613	831	2109	772	264	1604
642	392	1905	775	975	1001
644	830	1907	776	24	0503
645	400	1801	778	968	0808
648	900	1813	781	308	2213
676	891	2208	782	307	2212
680	901	2210	783	306	2211
699	923	1303	792	177	0905
700	228	1304	798	131	0911
701	244	1305	800	128	0907
702	227	1306	813	160	1003
703	226	1307	817	47	0211
704	256	1308	822	390	1908

DMC	Anchor	Madeira	DMC	Anchor	Madeira
826	161	1012	989	256	1401
828	158	1101	991	189	1204
832	907	2202	992	187	1202
834	874	2204	993	186	1201
841	378	1911	996	433	1103
842	376	1910	3012	854	1606
890	218	1314	3021	382	1904
891	35	0411	3022	393	1903
892	28	0412	3024	391	1901
894	26	0504	3031	905	2003
900	326	0208	3033	388	1909
921	338	0311	3047	852	2205
922	1001	0310	3064	883	2312
943	188	1203	3078	292	0102
945	881	2313	3325	159	1002
947	330	0205	3341	328	0307
956	40	0413	3345	268	1406
957	52	0612	3347	267	1408
962	54	0609	3348	265	1409
963	23	0608	3350	69	0603
966	206	1209	3608	86	0709
972	303	0107	3609	85	0710
973	290	0106	3705	35	0410
976	309	2302	3706	33	0409
977	313	2301	3708	26	0408
987	244	1403			
988	257	1402			